Words
of a
Derbyshire Poet

A Collection

F. Philip Holland

Five-Bar-Gate Publishing

ISBN: 978-1-906722-12-8
Text copyright ©F. Philip Holland 2009
Illustrations copyright ©Pat Holland 2009

First Published by Five-Bar-Gate Publishing, ©F. Philip Holland, 2009.
For further information go to:
www.fphiliphollandpoetry.co.uk

Printed and bound by: Kingsbury Press,
Unit 13, Durham Lane, Westmore Park, Armthorpe, Doncaster, DN3 3FE
For further information go to:
www.kingsburypress.com

Distributed by Mayfield Books, Sheffield. 0800 834920

Five-Bar-Gate Publishing

Front cover: Parkhouse Hill from Stannery Lane,
Glutton Bridge, Derbyshire,
Photograph ©Linda Harry, 2009

Back Cover: View over the hills near Earl Sterndale, Derbyshire.
Photograph ©Yvonne Oates, 2009

Dedication

for Patty, with love

Acknowledgements and Thanks

To Linda Harry, a very special friend, who has worked extremely hard in bringing this book to life. This lady has the diligence of a terrier and the resourceful experience of a life lived well. She always gives the ultimate support to those that ask of her and is one of the most charming and loyal friends anyone could wish for.

To Sir Christopher Ball, for kindly agreeing to write the Foreword to this book. His measured and perceptive words, candid critiques and true friendship are deeply appreciated. His advice, opinion, quiet wisdom, disarming wit, but above all his love of poetry, are both encouraging and inspirational. Not only a greatly respected figure in the world of Education, he also wears the pseudonymical hat of the prize-winning poet, John Elinger, and doesn't have the word negative when asked for his support.

To Roger Elkin, for his professional input and staunch friendship. Any fellow-poet who willingly gives their time to share thoughts and ideas, mutually exchanges work-in-progress and comments honestly is a generous and true Ambassador for Poetry. As a well-known prize-winning poet and a Poetry Competitions Judge for many years, his literary lectures are a joy and privilege to attend.

To Peter Low, Alyson Phillips and Nicola Stacey for allowing me to reprint their personal reviews of my poetry presentations over the years during The Buxton Festival Fringe.

To my family and all other friends; for their love, help, humour and understanding of knowing when to keep out of the way... but, thankfully, never very far. Finally, especially to my wife, Patty, for her illustrations and for putting up with me ...not necessarily in that order. She knows what she means to me ...even if I don't always tell her as often as I should.

FOREWORD

by

Sir Christopher Ball

I first met Philip Holland at the re-opening of the Devonshire Dome in Buxton a few years ago. We talked. In a matter of moments we discovered that we shared a love of learning, of words, and of Derbyshire. We both write verse. And now we send poems to one another for encouragement and criticism. I am deeply honoured to be invited to write this Foreword to Philip's collection.

Those who read these words have done something right – acquired a good book. Now do another: read it, and re-read it. Poems need to be read more than once, if they are to yield up their full value. Start with a short, apparently simple poem like Loreta (p.41). It is a poem of place, describing Prague through the sounds of Loreta's twenty-seven bells. Notice 'carillon', a lovely rare word that sounds like its own meaning, and 'wrinkled' – the big surprise of this poem. Who would have thought (or dared) to describe the sound of church bells as 'sweet, noble, wrinkled'? I also like the phrase 'marks time', with its double meaning of 'indicates the hour' and 'pauses' – like soldiers marking time. The form is regular (8,7,8,7 syllables), cemented by a single rhyme. Poetry repays close reading.

Next, try something longer and more challenging – Jazz in the street (p.61), perhaps (one of my favourites). This is free verse: don't look for regular form, but think about the verse-paragraphs (there are 16) and the line-breaks, for example ' "*Summertime*" / came floating down the street, / hidden by the press …', and the repetitions ('and kept appointments', 'and missed appointments', 'and forgotten appointments'). The craftsmanship is masterly, and the loving description of the busker together with a precise evocation of feeling is astonishingly well done. Each time I read it I am moved by this poem. Now re-read it, forgetting what I have written about it, and find your own realisation of it. Poetry requires re-reading.

Philip Holland is obviously a poet of place – and also of people. His native Derbyshire provides a backdrop for the more exotic locations of the second section (Abroad and Afar). His nature poems are superb, revealing the keen eye (and ear) of the countryman, and the farmer's affectionate familiarity with plants and animals (as in Charlock, p.16, or Hedgehog, p.49, or Heron, p.148).

4

For this poet, it almost seems that the life of nature is as full of character and interest, and as intimately known and cherished, as the humans he writes about. But not quite. If you are ready to be moved more deeply, read <u>What will you keep of me?</u> (p.79) or <u>Wave</u> (p.86) or some of the <u>Love Poems</u> (pp.151-157). Try reading them aloud. Poetry demands to be heard.

The author's range is remarkable. These poems demonstrate an astonishing variety of topics, genres and forms. There are poems about shoes (p.69), stones (p.87) and ashes (p.93), home and abroad, love and war, times and seasons; serious and comic verse, lyrical and descriptive poems, ballads and dramatic monologues; free verse and formal poems. Look for the many well-constructed sonnets. (I have found no less than seventeen; there may be some I've missed.) This is a form he handles with great skill and sensitivity. If you want to see what I mean, read <u>To Music</u> (p.59) – and then start searching for the others. As you read, make a selection of your own favourite poems from this rich collection (as I have done) and try to learn some of them by heart. Poetry enriches memory.

One other thing: every reader will recognise the author's love of the things and creatures and people he writes about. But you might miss the poet's delight in words, the raw material of our craft. Look at the first poem in the book, <u>Four</u> (p.13). This is, in fact, a series of four haikus, a rather strict form invented by Japanese poets, requiring three lines of 5,7 and 5 syllables respectively. (Count them!) But notice also the exuberance of the vocabulary: 'resplendent', 'may-fly glutted', 'corn-carrying', 'ormolu' (which I had to look up in the dictionary!), 'biting shadow', 'stiff and skeletal'. Here is a poet not afraid to use rare words, and skilled in the construction of telling phrases. Some of the poems are at one and the same time celebrations of their subjects – and of the richness, beauty and diversity of the words of our language (for example, <u>Cat</u> (p.55) or the several poems in the local dialect of this White Peak Poet, scattered throughout the collection). Poetry rewards careful study.

What more can I say to the reader who has patiently followed me thus far? Only this: I wish I could write poems as good as the best of these.

Christopher Ball

P.Holland.

Introduction

I offer these poems and prose to make up a collection which I hope will illustrate my fascination with, and love of, words.

I try to write what I know about; whether through the influences of the various stages of my life and work, what I have seen, heard or felt, or of where my flights of fancy have taken me.

Only through words; descriptive, reflective, observational, philosophical, comical and occasionally a few in my local Derbyshire dialect, can I endeavour to express and share my thoughts and emotions.

Sadly for me, I cannot draw, paint, sculpt, dance, sing or do anything else creatively. So, other than a little occasional piano playing, I am left with pen, ink, blank paper and words to form my particular kind of pictures, figures and sounds.

Sometimes these words are quite personal, for which I make no apology. Not everyone will enjoy all of them, but I hope most people will relate to at least some of them.

Living and working as a farmer in the White Peak for most of my life has certainly coloured my outlook and helped to shape my character. Nature and the countryside way of life figure extensively in my writing. Any unusual dialect words are explained either at the side or the foot of those poems containing them.

Music, history, art, and literature in general are also vital stimuli for me. I do occasionally try to imbue my creativity with some historical or classical reference, not always successfully, but it is fun to try. Words already span many centuries in literature. I am not the first to re-arrange them to try to say something differently, nor will be the last.

Travel and experiencing different cultures has been another spur to my writing. A short glossary may follow one or two of these poems to help to clarify any obscure, ethnic or unfamiliar words.

For me, all poetry is better appreciated by being spoken aloud. This is when I believe the words can really come alive.

My wife, Patty, has let me include a few of her sketches here and there; these should certainly bring a source of pleasure if the writing fails to.

Anyway, if I can briefly communicate with those who read these words then I am happy to have written them.

Some people say that you only write for yourself. I don't think so. Words are for everyone.

F. Philip Holland.

7

CONTENTS

Music and Memory

Observations and Contemplations

War and Warriors

Rap parody on "Kubla Khan" by S. T. Coleridge

for John and Sally Williams
for Philip Worthington
for Jackie Corrigan
for Deborah Hood

for Janet, because she likes owls
for Vicki Nottingham
remembering Mrs. D. Hambleton

for Patty
for Patty
for Patty

for Dr. Deborah Mutch

for Barbera Edwards

for Roger Elkin
for Wendy Ball

'Bonny' and 'Dog'

- Times and Seasons -

Four

Rushing green, full-sapped,
gives dawn a resplendent surge,
brooding shells take flight.

The buzz of honey
and may-fly glutted river
sing to lover's knot.

Corn-carrying sun,
that sinks and paints the canvas
red and ormolu.

A biting shadow
hungers in the empty land,
stiff and skeletal.

April

Young April, maiden of the year, with naïve smile
now shows her flimsy peeping green, pubescent, shy.
Escapes that voyeur, Winter, locked too long a while
in prison of his sullen, cold, myopic lie.

Her yellow laughter echoes on the coltsfoot's bank,
re-echoes to the softer cowslip's hanging crag.
Their lime and lemon shun the woodland's mossy dank,
which finds a sweet content in violet's purple brag.

The nibbling ewes move lighter on the pasture's frim.
Their patient winter-sleeping bellies' fruit now race
beneath the ash-tree's solemn shape. So gaunt and grim
and whipped by sudden scud of snow that leafless space.

Bold rooks march sanctimoniously from heap to heap
of unspread dung, in stoic search of wriggling life.
The bright, chill sky awaits the swallow's arcing sweep,
as urgent pigeon puffs his chest in search of wife.

In changing times of husbandry the farmer toils
on broken walls. Unmeasured by his length as yet,
he notices the mowdywarp's black velvet spoils,
reminding him once more that Spring does not forget.

P Holland.

frim – The particular green vibrancy associated with Spring grass.
The third verse makes allusion to what in Derbyshire are called 'lambing storms'.
These are light flurries of snow that seldom last very long, marking the death-
throes of Winter coupled to the birth of Spring. A local maxim runs: "When March
'as come 'n gone, snow'll melt on a cowd ston'." – cold stone.
mowdywarp – A mole.

Wet Afternoon

A bumper crop of psychedelic mushrooms
above a mingling herd of anoraks.
Fat babies in their plastic bubbles snoozing,
their anxious mothers follow three-wheeled tracks.

Victorian row of stolid, sandstone terrace,
with fluffed and moulting pigeons window-ledged.
Smart fashion boots now ruined by the splashing,
sad, empty shops that once were meat-and-vegged.

The drunken grid keeps gargling on the downpour,
by postman's last collection, five-fifteen.
Tanned promises of palm tree's shaded languor,
from travel-agent's window-neon scream.

Two grey, old ladies timid-skirting puddles,
rude-splashed by turbo-driven, tattooed yob.
A grimy bus that spews out all its riders,
then swallows more with frantic, hissing throb.

The town hall hides in dull-draped face-lift scaffold,
by regulation planted drooping grey.
The trader hopes, while wiping down his counter,
tomorrow will be better than today.

In streetlights rising colour schoolboys swagger,
defiant to the chilling Autumn blur.
A scowling cat on leeward side of dustbin
awaits the 'coming home' to dry its fur.

The waitress rubs the 'specials' off the blackboard,
which tempted no-one in to sit and lunch.
As traffic warden grimly rounds the corner,
to clock off early, shoulders in a hunch.

Commuters flood from last train's city service,
all eager for the Lottery's weekly draw.
The busker closes up his violin case,
and shuffles to the hostel's back-street door.

Charlock

She dreams for a year, or ten, or more,
this simple, humble weed,
this teasing beauty,
this huckrel!
And when we plough,
back she comes,
a feather-green shoot,
persistent now.
Kissed awake by lifting iron,
caressed by the coulter, spinning slow,
urged with the harrow's dance,
and rolled in the tilth, to grow.
And when we sow,
she is up already, drinking in the rain,
quivering in her wind-blown freshness,
her pale flowering again.
And when we frown,
she laughs, and sings her delicate scorn,
knows no denial of her children's children
yet unborn.
And when we mow,
she disappears,
with all her green and yellow,
and hides, and sleeps, and dreams.
Waits for a fanfare
of blundering hooves,
the next heave of the share.
Who does not dream
of their lover's next kiss?
What harm
was there?

charlock – Wild mustard, (Sinapis arvensis), the seed of which may lay dormant for many
years, but will quickly germinate at any subsequent ploughing.
huckrel – Derbyshire dialect term for a young woman who might be described as, if not of
doubtful morals, then of questionable virtue.
share - The shortened form of ploughshare.

16

Scything Thistles

The sun had warmed the day,
the blade, my back,
and, with the bullston', honed the weapon's edge
to hiss a battle-brightness.
Such quaint, old rhythm keenly learned
in days of youth, ago.
The curving wooden sneath,
smooth comfort to my hands,
its handles polished, and campaigned.
While overhead, just one delirious skylark
cooled the heavy air with tumbling ice of song,
to drench the hillside's humming saxifrage
in urgent, fresh reveille.

So, now to war on ranks of stubborn thistles,
that most rebellious weed and foe alike.
With swinging hips and arms
my vanguard started on,
each step to season's ready felling-time.
Rich yellow splashed the rocks
from vibrant stonecrop,
and harebells quivered in their fear.
As blows grew stronger with each slicing cut
the purple bonnets fell
in swaths of toppling death.
Like Cumberland, no quarter asked, or given.
Culloden echoed through the silvery, wind-blown grass.
With sweating neck and aching spirit's grateful cease,
on turning, none stood tall.
The field was won!
A raddled sunset cried of dying wounds,
and one far curlew wailed a last lament.

bullston' - *Carborundum sharpening stone, twelve inches long, tapering to each end.*
sneath – *The curving, wooden, two-handled shaft of a scythe.*
raddle -*Red ochre smeared on the ram's chest at 'tuppin' time' to mark those ewes which
have been mated. Historically, in The Peak District of Derbyshire, the rough calculation to
determining the main event of Springtime was: "If tha turns thi tups to a' Bonfire nayht,
tha'll gyet thi lambs onth' furst o 'April."*

"No se me daba cuido...me hago cargo queha sio...y a lo pasaito pasao"

Corrida en el cielo (*Bullfight in the sky*)

Cold dusk flows
in its deepening blue,
and grips my eyes in nearly-frost remorse.
And from the quiet trees
a hundred Spanish black-laced fans
stretch out an ovoid carapace of peace.
Spirits of the day,
alien and irregular, are silenced.
Shaded lights, borrowed by our lives and loves,
our thought's ramblings,
are blinks of days and nights uncounted as I walk.

Now come rainbows,
yet straight, like arrows, un-curved promises,
reflecting the last blood drops of a buried sun.
Bands of purple, under-lit by memories,
frost-fired divergent parallels, wasting in this chilling hour.
Livid scars across the thinning tautness,
weals on weals of clouded pain.
and the sweat of thrilled, cold fear.
So near that I could touch,
so far as makes no difference.

As yet, no stars appear.
Only from the pinpricked windows,
and the haunting of another time,
rekindles in the sky.
There is no hint of ease.
Dried, stroked and soothed in numbing frost,
the arteries of twigs, sap short,
hang silent as the plumès of goading banderillos.
Clawed on the solid flesh, massed and mute.

Far off, the looming black-bruised hill
becomes a bull, crowd roared,
passion bleeding, torn by cruel barbs,
arching, full-blooded, to the scarlet cape of night.

Striations, lances cloud-coagulate,
ice-form on the vivid blueness,
hovering and pitiless.

Then I recall a faraway brash fanfare,
and a staggering on the rim of earth.
The fatal sword is poised,
reaches to the thundering heart,
and sacrifices.
The scalding roar is silenced by an echoless saeta.
Legs crack in defeat, snap, drop and fold,
as life extinguishes on the raw blackness of the land.
Did I really see again that fire,
burning itself out, tortuously,
from the memory of that other time?

The frost fastens down,
drains the life, splits the rock
and mortifies.
Silence; ultimate and pulseless,
in the ignominy of pride.

And then, above,
a jewelled spirit flickers through;
Taurus, fixed, transfigured
high above the earth's ignoble bier.

What lead me to these memories, these ramblings?
Some distant solea?
This branding on the catafalque of frosted night?

I didn't mind
I knew it was just a dream
and past things are past.

The last stanza is a loose translation of the epigraph.
saeta – Traditionally, an unaccompanied Spanish religious song of great intensity, mournful
power and dramatic charge. Also has the connotation of a piercing dart.
solea – An Andalusian gypsy term signifying loneliness. Adapted from 'soledad', meaning
profound melancholy

Ash Tree

Once, long ago, this ash had satin dress,
with swags of keys all richly-hemmed in frills.
The last to clothe in leaves her nakedness,
a Salome of these wind-ravished hills.

That sapling, young and new to woman-hood,
danced playful, proud, no adolescent she.
Sure–footed in the rocks, her slender wood
then rose up. Graceful, lithe arms flowing free.

Her fingers now have loosed the veils of green,
like sensual dancer from Arabian sand,
her age revealed. Late frost denuded, seen,
and silhouetted black by Winter's hand.

Rememb'ring her when we were both in youth,
now broken, dying, in the storms of truth.

Autumn leaves

Children of the sapping season
full glow in blaze of mad defiance
to the bellows of the stripping wind.
Tired of blush at primping Spring
and green correctness Summer's fete,
now put on the fires of make-up,
red sashes and vermilion ribbons.
Invite the final party of the year
that calls the tune of tarantelle.

In laughing craziness they fly,
drunk by colour's cocktail draught,
in vortex of their host's request
to join in one last lustful spin.
By crisping, crackling flames of fun
they run and leap in circus spirals
shaking off their parent's fingers.
Showering sparks of rusty rouge
in celebrating masquerade.

And how the wind enjoys their paces,
encouraged in his hot pursuit.
He lifts and throws them, spangling skywards,
then rolls them cross the twisted roots.
Drifts their ripened, gaudy dresses
in gorged and glutted sex and sweat.
And now the naked shivering branches
see his ritual dance expended.
Shocked and spent they know again
their skeletons of Winter sloth.

The blustering tyrant, bored and sated,
sullies off in careless shrug,
leaves his million dancing partners
limp and damp in jilted heaps.
The weeping rain then lulls them earthward,
smoothes their fret in withering mould,
hums a cooling, sleeping quietness,
pours their golden vintage dew.

21

"I hope to see my Pilot face to face,
when I have crost the bar"

Alfred Lord Tennyson

Sunset

Surge, and surge, the little boats
turning to the evening's pride,
spray, and spray, the gilded swells
lifting to the final tide!

Gaze, and gaze, the scalded eyes
scanning far horizon's line,
haul, and haul, the salted ropes
harvesting the netted brine!

Sound, and sound, the blizzard gulls
crowding on the motion's flow,
groan, and groan, the ghosted hulls
echoing from the depths below!

Drop, and drop, the feathered sail
tiring of the skimming breeze,
sink, and sink, the blacksmith sun
floating on the last ebb's ease!

Fade, and fade, the headland rise
standing to the embered flood,
mass, and mass, the darkling skies
reaching to the feet of God!

Haymaking

A fine dew-mist on the break of the dawn,
the blarting of sheep on the hill, new-shorn.
Rich coloured hedges, wild duck in full-flight,
quivering grasses on cutting blade bright.
Flash of the river through valley's green lush,
quick-scampering vole and a gleaning thrush.
Tines spinning round in the blur of the swoth,
stirring the drone of the bee with the moth.

Shimmering heat on the field's stubble bare,
the comforting smell of the pollened air.
Seed-prickling weight of the crisp, new-baled hay,
creaking the gormers of old, four-wheeled dray.
Snapped-off ash leaves on the load's topmost row,
a sweet, cooling ride in the sunset's glow.
Welcoming pause of the wicker-work tea,
enamelled mug in the bole of the tree.

Sparks shooting high from the tractor's exhaust,
patient cows cudding, their milking late-caused.
Lifting the fork to the height of the loft,
glimpse of the owl in the old lambing-croft.
Sound of the hasp on the picking-hole door,
a great, yellow moon on the heather moor.
Washed, aching limbs in the starred evening's dim,
the peace and joy of an old harvest hymn.

blarting – The sound of ovine confusion at shearing-time when some lambs get parted
temporarily from their mothers. When all the flock is released back onto the hill, it takes a
few hours before all the 'families' sort themselves out!
swoth – The row of cut grass that is then made into hay by the drying sun and the tines of
the 'tedding' machine.
gormers – The upright gate-like structures at each end the hay cart to keep the crop
contained in transit.
dray – A four-wheeled hay-cart.

Rain

Today, the rain,
falling, dripping, splashing, crowning
the garden, the trees, the tiles.
Umbrella clouds that cling round the town,
down from the moors with blackening frown.
The bridges, the banks, the stiles
washing, pouring, churning, drowning
today, the pain.

Today, the rain,
brimming, swelling, oozing, seeping
the courses, the ponds, the hills.
Bright cold droplets that steadily fall,
join with the next in windowpane scrawl.
The hedgerows, the dales, the rills
running, streaming, pooling, weeping
today, the pain.

Today, the rain
bouncing, clinging, drumming, straining
the gutters, the butts, the dales.
Shimmering drips that fall from the leaves,
damp the edges of pocketed sleeves.
The mountains, the plains, the vales
dreading, knowing, tasting, draining
today, the pain.

Today, the rain,
dancing, flowing, surging, filling
the ditches, the dykes, the lakes.
Glistening wet beads that fall down my face,
fresh and salty that mix in the race.
The fences, the walls, the stakes
wetting, lapping, streaking, spilling
today, the pain

Today, the rain
brooding, bursting, howling, stinging
my cheekbones, my nose, my ears.
Soaked to my skin, in water-logged shoes,
numbed by the cold, with nothing to lose.
My heartache, my loss, my tears.
wringing, fretting, touching, bringing
today, the pain.

Autumn Times

Give me a heap of leaves, russet and crimson and gold.
Give me a faraway year, of dragons and knights so bold.
Give me the dangerous, crackling path, the towering trunks between,
with ramparts and drawbridges, horses and steel,
of my magical childhood scene.

Give me a heap of leaves, yellow and copper and brown.
Give me a lingering day, for lovers to smile, or frown.
Give me the sweet-smelling thorn, the burgeoning fruit of the vine,
with kisses and promises, tokens and signs
of two hearts, one yours, one mine.

Give me a heap of leaves, mottled and withered and old.
Give me a querulous hour, to prepare, to wait, to fold.
Give me the comforting dusk, the unfinished page to write,
of memories and records, hope and regret
remembered, but out of sight.

P. Holland

Inspired by D.H. Lawrence's poems in "The Plumed Serpent" section of his 'Collected Poems' and also integrating a poem by Fiona Crothall.

Ode to Light

A colour unknown
in its alien dimension,
illuminating strange wonders.

Soon will come Quetzalcoatl, in a brilliant blaze!
Prism burning, under shrouds of millennia,
distorting Time's unseen perimeter.

As yet, it is the hour of obscurity,
the hour for hunting, the hour of the jaguar.
His silvery image bends and quakes,
his merging shadow creeps
beneath the gilded host,
casting off the last creation.

The fire-light hurtles,
piercing the ancient mantle
with dawn's radiant eye.

I am the rainbird!
I am the Inca dove!
I am the peacock of a thousand eyes!
Reflecting back the orb of day,
and greeting all the Ambassadors of the morning!

I am the heart of whiteness.
I am a colour unknown to you.
I am a colour you have not even dreamed of.

And when he comes,
Quetzalcoatl, he, the feathered serpent,
you will feel his light,
you will see him in his glory,
you will watch and know the coming of his fire,
yet not be blinded by his colours!

And in his mantle will shine the fireflies!
And from his head a thousand torches!
And in his eyes the burning coals of Chichen Itza!

An etalon, a very Age of Light!

Quetzalcoatl – "Feathered Serpent" - An Aztec deity, joint originator of the cosmos.
Chichen Itza – A Mayan centre of religious and cultural buildings in the Yucatan.

Night Feast, Day Famine

An obese, belching moon
slices the rich clouds of night,
then pours transient, silver-jugged cream
lightly over each black-cherry portion,
as they pass succulently beneath.

An empty desert plate,
with a shallow spoon of dried-up river
scraping the empty pottery banks of hard-baked clay,
dusted with crumbs of wind-blown sand,
salt-burned by the grill of the sun.

A foggy day

The road is familiar, yet strange.
On any other day the land would stretch
and move easily beside the car,
come to meet us, and disappear behind.
Rolling underneath, a mirror to our movement,
A small convex of earth, well known so long.

But not today; today the fog has dropped.
The windscreen, like some bizarre contact lens,
is floating on a vast, blind iris of infinity.
We know what should be coming towards us,
We are sure what we will be leaving behind.

But not today; today we are in fog.
A confounding cataract on our knowledge.
We see some yards, then a gradual vapour-barrier,
perfectly circumscribed, parabolically numb,
as far as the eye can see, or rather, as the eye can not.
We are moving inside a small-measured globe of clarity,
driving slowly in a vast, undrowning sea of gas,
inert and silent, and poisonous only to sight.
We are held within some monstrous, opaque, white darkness,
inside the hideous eye of a blinded Cyclops.
Moving under the face of the world's driest sea,

We are infinitesimal, obscured,
a tick in the vast wool of the universe.
An atom in a limitless pile of rice.
Our pinprick of clearness, trapped by its own false horizon,
is held in the eye of a still-born storm,
a whirling dervish frozen inside a ball of glass.
We are in a shell without a yolk.
Silently brooding in a sphere of cold smoke,
hissed from some deep-frozen volcano,
held in amorphous, sustained suspense.

No matter how hard we peer into it,
No matter how we try to touch it,
The fog is always out of reach.
It slips through our fingers,
and our minds perception.
There is no sense
of being at all.

Winter

The one-legged ducks on the solid lake,
      the diamond glint from the barb-wired stake.
The lop-sided grin on the snowman's face,
      the still-born rosebud that lost the race.
The dripping swords of the guttering's guard,
      the feast on the bird-table, frozen hard.
The razor-white ferns of the cottage pane,
      the morbid rook on the church tower vane.
The clogged-up fleece of the Swale in the drift,
      the icy plop from the twig's sudden lift.
The frenzied yap by returning stick stilled,
      the dull, level dykes, grey lava filled.
 The lead-sullen lode of the north wind's flow,
      the defiant riposte of the snowdrop's show.
The freezing rime on the broken beech bough,
      the empty land, now too hard for the plough.
The tracks of the fox round the hen-house door,
      the ominous quiet that strangles the moor.
The plastered palings of the manor's fence,
      the desolate marsh in fog of suspense.
The fur-lined gloves that were dropped in the snow,
      the mercury warning, finger at low.
The flight of the geese to the estuaries host,
      the crunch of the boots with the Christmas post.

- Abroad and Afar -

Dawn

Ibiza, 6-30 a.m.

The blue-grey night, moon-sulking, ends her dream,
in fear, she hides behind the rock-rimmed earth.
While trembling sea contracts in silent scream,
and pushes from her womb in crowning birth.

Then, slowly rising out, the blood-disc shows.
The purpling clouds, as midwife, lift him free,
their edges gilded peach. Burnt-orange flows
a shining zig-zag line that reaches me.

On fecund palms, rich fruit above my head,
the lizard, yellow-fired, primeval, bright.
Hibiscus flowers, with petals dripping red
like burning silk, glow vivid in delight.

On timeless sand I greet the molten day,
beneath new waves my footprints melt away.

P. Holland

The Young Waitress

Windscreen wiper hands, and flashing eyes
that look each day to Tuscany's tall trees,
and olive tasting skin.

She is proud, legs patterned in uproarious lace
that coyly mocks suspicion of virginity.
She has the look that says woman.

She flirts and smiles, and writes it in your heart,
and on her pad, your order.
Smiles again, repeating "cold milk" with false importance.

Gives the table-cloth a delicate sweep of gold-encrusted fingers
that lasts just a little too long, and yet, too short.
An almond eyelid sideways glance, too quick, observed.

October sunshine, warm enough, floods through the ageing leaves.
The guests delight in urging eating is for life itself,
hospitable in culture's fair exchange excess.

"Bresoala, rocket e grana padano",
put down in grandest flourish,
and obligatory, later, her iced dessert.

The coffee,… hot,… intense.
Her spirit,… hot,… tasted.
But not for me.

I put down too many euros in confusion.
She gives me a tip I already know,
I read it in her eyes,… too old.

Memory is a fool, and gladly I am real again.
"Ciao, Pistoia!" Arrivederci to my dream,
while in the corner sits her beau, scowling, and young.

I envy them their lack of years,
their joy, their days and nights.
But not their coming pain.

31

The Pool

Around the pool, lines of bodies lying,
rows of tired business-men, elegant wives, young children.
All lazing, reading, anointing their flesh with lotions.
Reading the airport novel, the comic, the fashion magazine,
the daily stimulation of tabloid exposé.
Flattened and contoured plastic sun-beds cradling them,
lissom, excessed and re-constructed..

Then, carefully through the indulgent crowd,
they came,
a different, curious trio.
The crowd ignored them, not wishing to waste
one precious minute of paid-for pleasure.
Their guaranteed sun high in the guaranteed sky.
The expensive watering-hole of shaped concrete
and blue mosaic, lit in the evening, and chemicalled.

They arrived at the edge.
Father, mother, and child.
Three in a family, like so many more.
Come to enjoy the soothe and caress of the water,
the rejuvenating pool.

The father, older than most, by considerable years.
Grey haired, lined face and gentle.
She, older than her years, worn, yet serene,
and having that special grace seldom seen nowadays.
Their child, perhaps fifteen, or even thirty, who knows?
His years were difficult, his wheelchair witnessed that.

The crowd pretended not to see, like me,
reading, dozing, lying,
soaking in the intense afternoon of heat and indolence.

They lifted him out of his wheelchair, so carefully, so gently,
his thin legs hanging, the skeletal, useless arms,
His lolling too-big head, with rolling marbled eyes.
The mother took his weight so easily in her arms,
used to his slight chest and non-existent buttocks.

She held him, like a light, white corpse, with thin, dead limbs.
His trusting eyes stared across to me, and I looked away,
unnerved and strangely guilty.

Slowly, with encouraging sounds, she lowered him to his father,
already waiting in the water.
And he was offered, gently, softly, into the sparkling pool.
His eyes shone, great unblinking globes of sheer joy.
The thin, unspeaking lips drawn back in an ecstasy.
His teeth too big, his gaping mouth and lantern jaw
a piteous, soundless motion of dumb and noble animality
The arms useless in will, except to hang.
His father played him in a slow, arcing, gentle rhythm.
baptising him in the pleasure of the sparkling blueness.

The crowd held back, pasted on their hired boards like fish.
Disconnected fish,
not comfortable to share the awkward moment.
their precious bodies, uncontaminated, slab-lying,
perfectly proportioned, evenly tanned.
And so shockingly resentful in their good-mannered indifference.

The father bore him up, out, away from the jealous water.
Mounting the shallow steps so easily,
carrying his son's body, the legs hanging,
the long arms with too-big hands.
And his son's face, a vacant face,
was a shining moon of joy,
a thrilled silence.

The father laid him across the waiting mother's knees,
and moved away.
The shrouding towels enveloped,
her arms cradled.

Not even the *Pietà* looked so beautiful.

'Pietà' (1499) - By Michelangelo in St. Peter's Basilica.
Carved when he was 24 years old, this Renaissance masterpiece in marble depicts the body
of Jesus lying across The Virgin Mary's lap after the Crucifixion.

Garden in Winter

The dawn-light pulls my senses back from sleep's long hug,
and floods this strange, new garden for my blinking eyes.
The leopard-purring blanket licks it's whiskers in approval,
as, smiling back, I slip from underneath and face the day.
From off the flashing pool, reflected arrows pierce the panes,
and back-lit, sharpened plants shoot orange fires.

Dulled rhythms of some hidden dove keeps gentle time,
the raucous interspersing of the louries asking "*Where?*"
Dried, fallen leaves lie under trees' sad, resting boughs,
incongruous against the fleshy green of palms.
A weakened sun lights up the purpling-red of clinker brick,
as distant dogs bark warningly to keep away.

Across the lawn a woman walks in quiet, purposed stride,
she stoops, and then moves swiftly from the jetting mists.
The heightened colours blend and cry in joy anew,
luxuriant shades of '*yesterday, today and soon tomorrow*'.
A full-blown rose in memory of another season nods,
its roots held firm in rich, red earth's deep love.

lourie – *The South African grey turaco. Also known as the 'Go-away' bird. It's harsh call
can sound either like 'go-waaaay' or 'wheeere?'.*
*'yesterday, today, tomorrow' (Brunfelsia uniflora) – A plant which changes colour in it's
flowering - deep purple on the first day, lilac on the second and white on the third.*

34

Burg al Arab

Heat shimmering on the blue flatness,
a lone sail hoisted
without a wind in the dawn's quiet.
Spirit of the past, this ghostly dhow
voyaging nowhere, embalmed,
cast in concrete of the future's dream.

A shape of history reborn, re-designed the same,
spice-cargoed and gilded,
a vessel forever anchored, straining to the steel.
A bird alights on the crows-nest platform,
kerosene-feathered, paradised,
and trades a foreign tongue of cash for oils.

The past has leant its hand to imaged hope and won,
seven-starred Araby,
its marble fused with aromatic decadence.
The abra boats chug busily between the souks,
the palms in lines,
as desert roses wilt in sulphured smog.

Fantastic mirage of the architect's bizarre fades,
then clears in moonlight,
and the Bedouin turns away from his rugs.
The sand's lucre has bled away its mystery,
the Arab stallion becomes turboed horsepower,
even the camels have curled their lips and left.

Silicon chips denounce the Khayyám's Rubáiyát,
and now Armani rules.
Fitzgerald would have wept.
Yet the world will come and marvel at this place.
where tomorrow is built today,
where the spirit of man unleashed is undenied.

An oasis of liquid gold,
this elite ghetto, forever thirsty.
Ozymandias would have approved.

Song of the still-born child   *New Zealand*

It hangs on my wall,
a carving in kauri, primitive and strange.
A still-born child robbed of its life.
A talisman so strong that even now I am uncomfortable
to look at it for long. It has a power.

haere mai!   haere mai!   haere mai!
listen to the voice of Herewini!
            listen to the waters of Waitangi!
                listen, oh my children, to the sky!

It has a shape, half-fish, half-foetus.
An eye, cut from abalone shell, green of the river, blue of the sea.
The wood carved patiently, and given a voice,
a voice of the dead I cannot hear. The voice of a still-born child.

listen to the rustle of manuka!
            listen to the pulling of the waves!
                listen, oh my children, to the night!

The still-born has a special power, one the Gods must keep from men.
Tane Mahuta, who forced apart his parents in their love,
was the first child to be born on earth.
And thence, through time, any still-born child is his gift back to the Gods,
A special child robbed of life.
A spirit of the river and the night.

listen to the feathers of the kea!
            listen to the growing of the pearl!
                listen, oh my children, to the wind!

There it hangs, not touching the ground, not defiled by life.
My piece of Aotearoa, reverently carved.
Its living wood shaped by living hands
into the most sacred artefact of death.

listen to the rolling of the mere!
            listen to the swinging of the poi!
                listen, oh my children, to my tears!
                            haere ra !

kauri – *A gigantic New Zealand hardwood tree, massively tall and broad.*
haere mai! – *A greeting of welcome, traditionally said three times.*
Herewini – *A much-revered Master-Tattooist of the 'moko'; a carved, as well as pricked, skin motif which was impregnated with vegetable dyes. Full body art of this tradition was common among Maori men, and especially on the chins of pubescent daughters of the tribal chiefs. The real moko was outlawed by the Pakeha (White Man) many years ago. Modern moko is carried out using conventional methods of tattoo.*
Waitangi – *The place of the famous Treaty between the Maori people and the Pakeha.*
manuka – *A hardwood tree much prized by the Maoris – the slender, straight poles of young trunks are used for defensive palisades around the villages.*
'Tane Mahuta' – *'Lord of the Forest', Son of the Sky-god and Earth-mother. This magnificent kauri specimen still stands in a protected forest to the north of Auckland.*
kea – *A large alpine parrot, dull green, with vibrant orange under-wing feathers*
Aotearoa - *'Land of the Long White Cloud' – Original Maori name for New Zealand*
mere – *A fighting club, carved from 'greenstone'; a form of nephrite jade.*
poi – *Balls of white flax hung on light rope, swung by women in Maori cultural dances.*
haere ra! – *Farewell.*

The Moon Tree   *Randpark, R.S.A.*

So white, these blossoms, icily blanched,
each hung from a graceful cocoon.
New-strewn, eclipsing the sun, entranced,
and born of the wandering moon.

Hanging, showering, pentagon shapes,
the shrouds of a mystical night.
Cambric, calico, coverlet drapes,
a white of the snow-goose in flight.

So white, these trumpets, and softly starched,
pale lights, with a cool, waning sheen.
Five-webbed, full-blowing, sun-bleached and parched,
a white of the palest, pale green.

Melting, tapering, candle-waxed glow,
faint-breezed with a whispering noise.
Veil-robed, time-slowing, dream-relaxed flow,
half-lit in a chandelier poise.

So white, these flowers, mist-floating high,
a white of candescent lime-dew.
Slender, magical, dropped from the sky,
and caught on the moon-tree for you.

The Red Sea isn't red.
It is the deepest cobalt blue.
It is a heavy, pungent, sonorous hue
That outweighs the gentian chiffon sky above.
It is a dyed, leaden sweep of shimmering coolness
That lifts up even the mountains of Jordan, opposite,
And floats them gently to the warm, winter-shining sun.
It is blue mercury, with a far-off crust of arid meerschaum,
Like the desert night holding up the craters of a nascent moon.

The Red Sea isn't red.
Now, a bolt of peacock silk,
That rolls, adjacent, in mystic train.
Merges from the outer-wedded profundity,
Flashing with silver coins of kisses from Herod's lips.
Belly dancing with the speckled eyes of seven-veiled Salome.
Liquid strata that moves seductively nearer in persuasive glances.
Drawn in by urgent pulling of the coaxing shallow's eagerness below.
Like the cool desert night yielding up to the strength of inevitable dawn.

The Red Sea isn't red.
Where the sea comes closer,
Where Egypt draws the deepness up.
A narrow eyelid strip of azure lapis-lazuli.
A single blueness that guards against the evil eye.
That keenly watches, as the noble desert hawk, for vermin.
Forever looking to some far-off horizon of the patient Sphinx.
Like her sightless, stony knowledge of watchful, vain-gloriousness.

38

The Red Sea isn't red.
Still closer comes a pale gem,
A sweet-wet turquoise, translucent,
And caught in the nets of the coral below.
Preciously setting the discernable waves in play.
A mosaic banding of light blue eggs that lie brooding,
Warmed into life from the mines of the ocean's antiquity.
A thousand million rippling cabochons of much-prized flotsam.
Like so many clusters of glowing dates hanging in the dusk of oases.

No,
The Red
Sea isn't red,
The Red Sea isn't red.
The blueness, almost gone,
So close, transcends to clearness,
Swimming transparently as gossamer.
It moves like a mist above the sleeping pebbles.
Then, in pity, laps lovingly towards the thirsty shore.
The salty moistness bathes away the harsh heat of years
In mirage, a moving ghost from some refracted looking-glass.
Now, the fine-ground sands of Pharaoh drink the blue blood of the sea.
In mirage, a moving ghost from some refracted looking-glass,
The salty moistness bathes away the harsh heat of years,
Then, in pity, laps lovingly towards the thirsty shore.
It moves like a mist beneath the sleeping pebbles,
Swimming transparently as gossamer.
So close, transcends to clearness,
The blueness almost gone.
The Red Sea isn't red.
Sea isn't red
The Red,
No.

Bernini   *Villa Borghese, Rome*

In the Villa Borghese I stand to stare
at two figures in marble, struggling there.
A malevolent Pluto and imminent rape
of fair Proserpina, in hopeless escape.
Molten, yet frozen, gorged, and shocked,
poised, pulsating, translucence locked.
His powerful arms in lustful embrace
held fast aloft her trembling grace.
Sinews draw tight his thick muscled legs,
she turns to flee and, weeping, begs.
His hands of iron pale flesh held tight,
the fingers viced on dimpled white.

His beard-brazen head, underworld-massive,
her moon-cold breast, delicate, passive.
The heaving torso sun-bursting bold,
she fails to deny his monstrous hold.
Mercy and might so unevenly dealt,
pure ice, the volcano will savagely melt.
The light is caught and, pearl-like, held
dramatic, or dimmed into shadowy meld.
Behind at their feet, the three-headed dog,
hideous, slavering and watchful, agog.
The horror is paused, but threat is still meant,
the crime unfulfilled, yet forever intent.

Such brilliance of the sculptor's skill,
does mind and heart and soul o'erfill.
The moment's passion, fixed in time,
so burns my eyes, confounds, sublime.

40

Masada

by The Dead Sea

In desert fortress shaped by Herod's hand,
impregnable, a palace dovetail-locked,
sweet-water cisterns filled, and stores full-stocked,
the Zealots take defiant, final stand.
As Silva's sullen patience soured to hate,
in bitter siege encircling freedom's will,
the rampant Romans built, now keen to kill,
since three long years of empty, thwarted wait.

The knowing, brave defenders watched the plan
unfold in brute, relentless legion scheme.
These few, undaunted, still in freedom's dream,
resolved their fate, heroic to a man.
So, each, in turn, slew daughter, son and wife,
Masada's men chose death in freedom's life.

Loreta

Winter in the Czech Republic

Loreta's carillon of bells,
that number twenty-seven,
sweet, noble, wrinkled sound of Prague,
marks time from earth to heaven.

San Filippo

Massed olive trees of San Filippo,
like antique candelabra,
still, in the drying clouds of morning,
folded by the brown-earth Tuscan hills,
with pregnant branches lifting,
dripping, blue-green waxen fruit.
Across, the brooding buff Castell del Nero,
half-hidden in its slender bars of cypress.
Along the slopes, a myriad vineyard wires
play symphonies of wine, unpicked.
Their silent scores the plangent music of the land,
sweet purpling-black, maestoso.

Faint monotone of rhythmic pigeons
gently ushers in a bright young sun,
to tease the peeling paint of closed, green shutters
and bleed mixed pungency
of rosemary and thyme.

Bleached, spiky grass awakes my sullen feet,
and leads me to a deepening seclusion,
yet quiet thrills aware, an inner peace.

Some late-roused cockerels
answer to each other's kingdom,
and from a distant, flat-topped tower
seven strikes remind this world
that all is well.

Certaldo Alto

Tuscany

Oh, we have seen your characters, Boccaccio!,
sat outside the tavern in your street,
your youths and maidens underneath an awning,
the sunshine in their smiles no rain could dim!

And we have drunk your robust, red Chianti!,
nearby your casa, on that ancient hill,
watched your gaudy, medieval pageants,
and listened to the shouts of gladdened men!

Oh, we have eaten olives and formaggio!,
fresh bread on friendly terra-cotta plates.
Followed in the thankful re-enactment
of deliverance from the ravages of plague!

And we have heard your church bells ring out boldly!,
watched your pavements thronged with eager feet.
Your people lived through all of this, Boccaccio,
their childrens' children still live here today!

Oh, we have run our lives as in the Palio!,
fought and cherished, burst our lungs and wept.
Laughed, repented, made the same disasters,
and lived each moment, if it were our last!

And we have read your moralising stories!,
weighed the twists and turns of mortal men,
who loved and lost, rebuked, denied, exulted.
Your women, pure and tainted, young and old!

Oh, would that we might see like you, Boccaccio!,
tell our words through lips that you breathed through.
Ten thousand times ten thousand words we'll struggle,
and none compare with your Decameron!

Giovanni Boccaccio (1313 – 1375). Italian Renaissance author and poet. "The Decameron"
– arguably the most famous book written by him, tells of three young men and seven young
women who flee to Certaldo to escape the plague in Florence.
The Palio - The famous horse race run annually within the main square of Sienna

My thumbnail pierces through the tough, thick peel and shrugs it off.
The zest reminds my nose of prickling, keen flamboyance from the tropic's flare,
and I can sense the heavy air where once this orange hung
suspended in the groves. A million yellowing rows
sun-cradled under Hartebeestport's mountain range. Young
Naartjies, navelled, ripening and asleep.

My mouth begins to salivate expectantly, the rolling tongue
held firm by sucked-in cheeks, the teeth on edge.
My fingers feel the latent heat of Africa.
Her soil, warmed by a southern disc of bronze,
now turned to magic, held in inner honeycombs of tender, frail, thin skin.

The centre, opened up and vulnerable within,
divides the segments in a crown, yet leaves them joined.
The jewelled juices, held in sheer, translucent, still-encapsulating sacs,
Tempting me to take them from the starburst plan, and slowly taste.

I pause, then ease just one soft part inside my mouth,
and gently squeeze
those first few drops of liquid, sharply sweet.

I will taste my orange slowly, savouring, and think about your garden,
and your birds of paradise.
and stare through glass dividing me from chilling rain, and you.

I will close my aching eyes,
and listen to the strange, wild sounds of Pilanesburg
and drink in all the sun.

Hartebeestpoort – The main citrus growing area north of Johannesburg.
Naartjies – A small type of orange, similar to a tangerine.
Pilanesburg – A massive game reserve in the R.S.A., near the border with Botswana.

- Animals and Farming -

Hare

Sleek, athletic scout, spirit of the high plateau.
Shy, brown watcher of the season's round.
Razor-sighted and radar-eared,
living in the dangerous open.
No dugout, trench or hole.
Relies on speed and
double-backed
manoeuvres
to live
and
lie.

Devoid of all aggression, save only to a rival jack.
Then, mad-cap boxer, in the dance of March,
runs around the does in tagging trains.
A vibrancy that marks the start
of Spring's bizarre campaigns.
Crouches in camouflage,
an earthy spy, alert,
then zigzags off,
confounds my
blundering
boot.
.

Shire-horse

Sleek-moving ponderous giant,
with jangling brass and brightened chains,
polished like a gypsy-bauble.
The red, cockaded, wired-on plumes,
like hideous peacock, plaited, splayed.
Rude truncheon-tail plucked bare, tied up
and artificial flower mocked,
makes clown this great colossus.

And yet his gentle, ancient eye still burns
a fire primeval. When, still a wild thing,
yet un-hindered, graced the plains,
the moors and dales his kingdom.

Which one first caught and hobbled?
Haltered, broken-in and trained?
Checked by strips of hand-stitched hide,
the spirit tamed, though never quenched.
Ploughed furrows, pulled the harvest's
wooden carts and Medieval-jousted.
Charged at pike-men, armour-plated,
dragged cannon, and condemned to gallows.
Hauled timber for a thousand ships,
draughted ale for thirsty workers.
Moved mountains with a simple rope
on towpaths by the quiet canal.

And now, so rare, this splendid Shire
sent one more time around the ring,
applauded now in second lap of honour.
Noble friend, your work is done,
endangered beast, as in a zoo,
and patted by a hundred hands.

A bygone age, sad memoried smells,
the clip of shoe on cobbled yard.
Soft muzzle snort and may in bloom,
my distant childhood dimmed.
The swingle-tree and rusty hames
replaced by stinking engine.

Now stallion ghosts and mares in mists,
shake off the centaur-half of man,
race back through centuries gone,
reclaim their wings of Pegasus.
Appalled to see their children's children
stalled and harnessed, judged and gelded,
shod in iron, shafted, flogged
and butchered for pet dogs.

Rhino

Krugersdorp, South Africa

A tawny bluff and a rocky road
and the winter Randsburg grasses.
The silent sun hammering down
in browning blows on the dying day.
The pitch and roll of the four-wheel-drive
and the red dust sharp in my nose.
Tensioned hands round binoculars
and my eyes at the eager ready.

A curving rise, a break in the scrub,
then I saw, and yet could not believe,
till a second glance found me staring.
Yet the beasts told me lies, so I thought.
They watched us steadily, watching them,
we knew honour to be in their presence.
A finger of warning, be still and look,
I thrilled to be granted their choice.

A female and calf, motionless, stood
lost in the oldest of landscape.
Myopic eyes stared back at my own,
lost in a wonder of time.

She moved, just so slightly,
and flicked forward an ear.
Her hide was a carving in granite.
The calf was her mirror,
though the horn a mere bump,
yet its youngness seemed old, as the mountains.

Their ancient bond of kindred blood
shone in a pre-history fire.

She snuffled and grunted,
and blew on her son.
He moved and entered her shadow.
Sweetest pain of protectiveness
was her soft armour of motherhood.

She lowered her head
and sifted the ground,
uneasy with alien smells.
The sun, not so harsh, now low in the sky,
yet still with a handcuff grip.

We moved on with the track,
the red dust blew away,
from the rawest
Madonna and Child.

Hedgehog

On the patio he trotted,
quicker than you'd think, and clotted
with a washing-line of strips of papered leaves.
A rugby shape of rolling spines,
some tiny, long-forgotten dinosaur that finds
himself a living proof that Darwin's theory achieves.

Thus, being the better part of valour,
curls defensively into a ball, plays dead, with pallor.
The terrier's intrigue, well-rewarded with a rueful yelp, perceives
this is no easy prey,
and that there is no other way
to make attack on that which, sure and safe, deceives.

He, after time, unwinds
his dry sea-urchin metamorphosis and finds
the white ceramic dish of milk I gave, and he receives
in grateful, snuffling laps.
I wonder if, this year, I should, perhaps
not gather up in withering heaps and burn the leaves,

lest he be roast alive.
Leave alone, let live, and thrive.
My prickly scourge of pests, in thanks, revives
a simple give and take.
A sharing of the quiet dusk and daybreak,
implicit in the universe, where each survives.

His table manner done,
sets off across the lawn in shuffling run
and briefly pausing by the potting-shed, relieves.
Dim shadows swallow,
as underneath the tipped-up garden barrow
he disappears in broken pots and crates. Believes

that he is safe, and must
have known that he has earned my trust.
So let the leaves cover, when one, the other, grieves.

The Calving

The crisp night air invades my lungs in full,
to clear my head of ash log's smouldering scent.
With jacket buttoned–up and hat down-pull,
then stride the yard to calving-box intent.

Eye put to finger-hole in ancient door,
and quietly watch the cow in labour's sweat.
She pants in straw deep-strewn across the floor,
the inner life makes her to push and fret.

Her time is come, that patience must repay,
to give, in spite of pain, another life.
She stretches out, and rolls her eye away,
the belly pumps, and nostrils curl in strife.

I quietly lift the rusty, forged sneck-latch,
and slowly enter in to her domain.
Speaking low, while paused beside the kratch,
"Sooo then, lass," her confidence to gain.

She raises up her head and flaps the ears,
and strains again, the flanks would seem to burst.
Once more she rests, in clouds of breath so fierce,
I sadly tell her, "That's not yet the worst."

She watches me as I reach up for rope
that hangs full-ready, high on oaken beam.
The strains come more, I kneel behind to cope,
and see the membrane's white-ballooning gleam.

My fingers feel two feet, and then a nose,
encased in gentle fluids warm defence.
And knowing from so many other shows,
that all is well, in spite of being so tense.

She senses now that I am here to aid,
our common purpose, mine in shallow part.
So nature's forces swell in complex grade,
a bond between us, natural in art.

The hide on her, soaked through, smells good and warm,
she bawls in effort grim, and holds the strain.
With ropes around the fetlocks' steaming form,
I pull, and then relax, when pressures drain.

"Wunce moer, mi lass," and then the head is through!
the calf, at me, then blinks a baleful stare,
"We'er winnin' nair, s' jus' keep pushin' true!"
She understands, though kicks out at thin air.

"Nair fer th' hips!" One last and gallant heave,
our push-and-pull together as a pair.
Taut ropes, teeth clenched, and aching muscles cleave,
the lesser from the greater beast to bear.

 The calf lies sprawled in wet and gory state,
relieved, I wipe the nostrils mucus free.
A gasp of air decides the future's fate,
to live, extend the root stock of the tree.

The dam then rises, anxious for her calf,
and licks the reason causing so much pain.
She's wary now, and then I have to laugh,
and back away, my herd increased again.

Her calf then tries to raise its sticky head,
and soon it will be up on wobbling legs,
to swollen udder, gorged, it will be fed.
"As fer mey? Nair bacon 'n fried eggs!"

kratch – a manger

The Slaughter

Scratch;
I'm not sure
when the word
came to be.
I know its use...
easing the way...
soothing the body into peace...
held still on this crude altar of wood.
All pain erased...
the savage sharpness over...
frenetic struggle becoming quiet...
blackening blood leaving the stark serenity of death.
Lying still now...
sacrificed on the rough-hewn pine...
conscience water washing away the trouble of life...
quick scraping the bristles away, taking off the hair shirt.
A last supper...
stretched out on a guilty table...
bled innocent, sloughed, a riven image...
Pale body cooling into wax-bloomed peace.
Drawn, halved...
thudded, dissected...
Later, shrouded in the winding muslin...
hook-hung in the dark cellar, eternally silent.
Completed...
scrubbed down...
all sins washed away...
from this killing-bench of raw necessity.
I'm not sure when the name came to be...
only my father telling me it was so...
But I know its use of dispatch...
A final deathbed into oblivion.
Quiet now...
except for the shrill echoing of a squeal...
heard in memory...
coming from the scratch.

Bat Ballet

Cocooned all day on belfry's barre,
  he hangs in gravity, at rest.
    Like eerie, venomous fruit, unpicked,
      that ripens with the evening star.
        The sunset leaves his louvered cage
          and purpled haze of shadows creep
        to deepen even more the smell of hay
      and dim the valley's summer stage.
    Fur-feathered sprite, half-bird, half-beast,
  with mawkish, leather-stretching wings,
he swoops his frantic debut dance,
  ecstatic in the meadow's feast.
    Through still, black tracery of dusk,
      a brief, erratic dot, too quick for tired
        eyes to plot his frenzied trance,
          intoxicate with pollen's heavy musk.
      A bleak, full-yawning moon, too big,
    lifts slowly from the shouldering hill.
    Backlighting boughs in silhouette
  to entr'acte his next mad jig.
To etch the blue-grey slumberous clouds,
  he dips and loops his secret signs,
    and scratches magic tableaux of delight,
      weaving like a wizard through the shrouds.
        Iron hoops of sun-soaked cartwheels sheer
          to black in cool of stack-yard's gloom.
      As now come dusty, sweating fetlocks,
    aching, plunging in the shallow mere.
    The old sweet-chestnut sweeps their matted manes
  with jagged lace, a dowager's mantilla sadly draped.
Sweet-soothed by chattering millrace flume
  their proud release from dray's bright chains.
    Still he skips his nocturne leaps in mad, rhapsodic play,
      those scorched, compliant killing-fields
        so glutted for his lunatic rampage,
          strafing stubbled acres reaped today.
      As night throws brume bouquets of dew in rapt recall,
    he vanishes through the hayloft's stone-ringed eye.
  Then re-appears to take his last, brief, mystic acclamation
in one wraith flourish of scuttering curtain-call.
  So ends Le Danse Diablo, choreographed in ancient rune.
    Applause of utter silence begs for more.
      Then, for his encore, scrawls a black and vivid lightning
        sorcerously across the globe of marbled moon.

Mr. Lawrence and his Mountain Lion

His words shook me,
grabbed up in their tender teeth,
held like a kitten,
unarguing,
firm.

I was young, not yet a man,
but stirred, attuned,
and impressionable.

Reading, for the first time,
a different kind of language,
haunting, beautiful
and sad.

His vivid view alarmed and seared my eyes,
the pitying questions and rich, wry commentary
agreed with,
and understood.

But what I felt the most was raw affinity,
like him.
In a wilderness that singularity transcended,
the silent tumult of life in all its frost and fire.
Savage simplicity against
the stacked-odds trophy men.

And I smelt the pine in thinnest, sharpened air,
And I saw her yellow eyes, mist-glowing dead,
I felt her tawny pelt grow cold beneath my hand.
and knew her pain,
and his.

Remembering now that shock of keen awareness,
its earthy pungency,
and the querulous whim.

His words imprinted,
like her spoor,
unforgettable,
burned,
iced.

Cat

Carpet-stretched and embers-warmed,
Whisker-washed and lissom-formed.
Door-jamb-scratched and jumper-caught.
Static-furred and Christmas-bought.
Mewling-mass of kitten-kindle,
Persian-crossed with old-tom-brindle.
Mincing-down-the-garden-walk,
Up-side-down with string-and-cork.

Spitting-snarl and bristling-fight
Through-the-caterwauling-night.
Gymnast-routine, back-side-licked,
Guilty-feathered, milkman-kicked.
Ankle-rub-insinuating,
Leapt-on-lap-ingratiating.
Rooftop-mating, "lost-and-found",
All-dog-hating, neutered, drowned

Garden-stalking, robin-twitching,
Parasitic-collar-itching.
Door-step-waiting-home-from-work,
Alley-way and dustbin-lurk.
Lucky-black, with nine-lives-living,
Sailor's back, nine-unforgiving.
Shrew-tormenting, mouse-hole-spied,
Empty-goldfish-bowl-denied.

Litter-tray or full-house-training,
Hates-to-go-out-when-it's-raining.
Banned from old-folk's-home-decree,
Tarmac-flat-catastrophe.
Pharaoh-honoured, broomstick-sat,
Patterned-on-the-front-door-mat.
Friend-for-life, apart-from-courting,
R.S.P.C.A.-reporting.

Now-we've-moved-into-a-flat,
Don't think we'll-get-another-cat.
Old-and-feeble childhood-pet,
Tiddles-put-to-sleep-by-vet.

P.Holland

Fox-trap

Down in my cellar is an old fox-trap.
Made of iron, forged, sprung into life,
by ancient, crafty, unknown hands.
A pair of jaws, snarling and keen,
drawn back in a smile of death.
Set by a feather-tension clip, so light,
on the bait-plate's tempting patience.
He will come tonight, the old dog-fox.
Made of sinew, he will spring into death,
by instinct, craft, and knowing eyes.
Drawn by the feather-filled coop of night,
with agile paws and flashing mask.
His teeth bared playfully back, so quick,
in the blood-bath's glutted frenzy.

But I must be more cunning than he;
a new lock fix, old timbers replace,
I must remember to shut up the fowls
before the red night comes to check.
His trap is set, baited with my neglect
and poised on a red hair-spring.
He knows it is only a matter of time,
I will be trapped by the inevitable mistake.
He can wait, and depend that some other
coop-keeper's guard will drop, if not mine.
He has baited his trap with forgetful contempt,
in the waiting un-stained snow.

The innocent fowls just nod and scratch,
nodding and scratching.
The old dog-fox then springs and snaps,
springing and snapping.
Their red feathers fly, even redder,
flapping and squawking.
His red fur blurs, even redder,
tearing and killing.

He has caught me in his fox-trap of patience,
this red-coated huntsman, killing for pleasure.
He has left me the horror of corpses and feathers,
though the feast was far more than the hunger.

So, my old fox-trap now is set, baited with revenge.
The tense jaws open and smiling, patiently waiting.
Till the red night returns,
and the snap.

Badger

Grey, gruffling, black and white,
Cold, snuffling, moonlit night.

Leaving sett underground,
Listen! owl's haunting sound.

Spring returns, yawn and scratch.
Sing cuckoo, new dawn hatch.

Summer heat, shearing flocks,
Smelling hay, blowing clocks

Autumn barley ripens soon,
Silver sickle, harvest moon.

Winter grim, snow and sleet,
Frozen lake, icy sheet.

Howling blizzard, drifting deep,
Hibernating........fast...   asleep.

The Gather

We set off, you and I, on a gather.
Two friends, one troubled, one not.
We went across an open field
leading to the spot you chose,
This time you gave the commands,
for once I simply agreed.

Two pairs of eyes, one misted, one not.
Gathered across the aching sky,
grey, wet clouds were crowding,
by a curlew's lamenting long cry.

Two sets of legs, one heavied, one not.
We went, you and I, with my burden
of you in a bag on my back.
We stopped, at the place, for the working,
not with a stick, but a spade.
And this time, I on my own.
Turning the turves to show
the welcoming, gathering brown.

Two pairs of ears, one listening, one not.
Across in the wood, the whistling wind
lifted the mourning crows, then folded
them back in the gathering tops.

Two hearts, one heaving, one not.
Laid low in the shrouding sack,
wearing, the only thing ever possessed,
the collar I could not take back.

We filled up the space, you and I,
the brown covered up by the green.
Across my face I drew my arm,
was it rain that spattered my cheek?
Or memory of a cold, damp nose,
that used to push up into my hand,
to gain the rough, good-natured pat,
lick my fingers and leave them wet.

I turned, and left you there,
to gather the flock

58

To Music

My scythe lies idle in my hand awhile,
and paused, I hear the sound of rising lark.
The silvered notes on echoing clouds beguile,
and lift my eyes from swaths of grass, dew-dark.
The full-blown summer's brass-melodious bees,
and harp from water-fall in mill-race glade.
Leaf-lifting rustle from harmonic trees,
and rhythm kept by sharpening of my blade.
From moor the curlew's melancholy horn,
and drumming hay-cart, drawn by horse-shoe beat.
The hill-side's distant call of sheep new-shorn,
cacophony of concert, playing sweet.
In Nature's chords, from God's conducting hand,
the glorious, simple music of the land.

Pavarotti

Silenzio!
Let all listen!
He is dead!
Let the strings be cut,
the brass stopped up,
the reeds become choked.
Let only a muffled drum keep time,
to echo a heart now stilled.

Lento lachrymosa!

His voice gave life to dumb, papered notes,
an instrument like no other.
His life, like all others, transient,
not always smooth, not always sweet.
Life that knew all the passions, all the sorrows.

Ah! but his voice,
so smooth, so sweet, and the power!

A voice has to experience life before it can sing about it.
Rudolfo, Don José, Pagliacci,
He was their voice, their chance to tell all.

Heaven has a new tenor, and Earth a hundred million thirsty ears.
Bravo! Bravo! Bravissimo!
Let all listen! Nessun dorma!

But now watch the jackals fight and gnaw over your bones.
Wait for the poison to pour from jealous mouths.
Listen to the dis-included-in-the-will howl,
and the earnestness of those who say they loved you best.

How shrill they sound.
You are better out of it, Maestro.

No more curtain calls.

Omni dorma.

Jazz in the street

"Summertime"
came floating down the street,
hidden by the press of shopping bags,
suits, detached faces, jeans
and late appointments.
Sweet melancholy, reverberating off the plate-glass,
softly, smoothly blowing away the reality of October.

And then I see him,
glued to his saxophone,
like an easy lover.
The outward performance, street-wise, sassy,
the private one, unseen, unheard.

My spine melts to their sounds
I sit on a bench near them,
like a voyeur, writing.
Vibrations, mind relaxing,
from a place far away,
some cellar, a smell of cigarettes, and sex.

He wears a grey jump-suit, slack and loose,
a green pork-pie hat, too big, in fun.
Jammed down, in fun, too big,
and the obligatory, long, black scarf
dropping to his toes, just
like his notes, dropping on the pavement, just.
His cassette player on a small speaker,
the carrying case lies open, with its coins, just.

He dances with her,
yet never moves a step,
holding her with tender-pressing fingers,
blowing kisses down her neck.
The cords of pressured veins rise up in his throat,
his cheeks balloon in love.
She sings for him, husky and low,
her brassy mouth open and sultry.

A man empties his cup down a drain,
screws the cup back onto his thermos,
and disappears into the crowd,
swallowed by the shopping bags,
Legs, worried faces, jeans,
and kept appointments..

Their song ends, sated.
He pauses, comes back from his hidden place.
He presses some key on the player,
"*Misty*" opening begins.
He lifts her up and holds her gently again,
gently to his lips.
No-one can see them.

The shopping bags pass by,
jeans, high heels, coats, wallets
and missed appointments.

Silence.
Only the sounds of people in October.

I ask his name,
"Sello" he answers, and spells it for me,
grins, wide enough to leap over,
his teeth like keys from an old piano,
eyes soft and dancing with slow rhythm.
I grin back,
and write more notes about him,
and his lover.

They sing again.
A young woman throws a few small coins,
some miss,
and roll around the pavement manuscript,
then lie like dull, copper crochets
and silver, shiny quavers,
like his notes, rolling again.
We pick them up for him, but he keeps playing,
eyes closed, oblivious.

The shopping trolleys trundle by,
anoraks, a zimmer frame,
newspaper under an arm.
Blank faces that don't even walk in his time.
The tape begins again.
A different world surrounds theirs.
He blows his very soul into her.

I get up, and move slowly to him,
He looks at me and our eyes trust.
I slowly place one fingertip on his neck,
and feel their sounds.
Her skin is yellow,
Covered in the sheen of seduction,
His, dark, as a dream.

The shopping goes by,
hands, unknown faces, purses
and forgotten appointments.

Silence again.

He asks what I'm doing.
I tell him I'm writing notes for a poem.
Can he have it?
Yes, if I meet him again.
He presses the player.

I walk slowly off, with my notes, and his.
Swallowed in October, and
"Summertime."

Orchestra

No.1 Strings

Pieces of wood, reshaped, glued and varnished,
brought back to life from prized, dead planks long stored.
When just young saplings, fretting and highly strung, as now,
the breeze riffled through their vibrant leaves, and sang.
Shading that very same horse from buzzing summer's heat,
whose proud, taut hair swishes again across the hollowed grain,
and bows above the vaulting bridge in limpid pools of sound.
The player, like a puppeteer, takes up and makes them dance.
The two parts touch and move in tender, subtle waves;
aping the sweet, mercurial, splintering joy of April's lark,
or deeply plumb and stir the ocean's sad sonority,
sounds brightly sun-sparked, then honeyed, full, in calm,
or darkly anger-menacing, then lachrymose in despair.
Then, finally, a pure contemplation of loving bliss.
The dumb instrument only living at the bow's caress,
and dying, he falls silent, when lifted gently from her.

No.2 Brass

Lumps of earth, deep dug with sinewed sweat and pain,
taken from the ancient, thundering edge of Vulcan's forge.
To yield from stubborn ore the metal's precious birth,
melted, fluxed and rudely poured to dull, deaf ingots.
Drawn and coaxed from resisting elemental distrust,
to flow and bend in ever-thinner complex coils and keys.
The brilliant, shiny serpents now open-mouthed and ready,
no deadly poison, then radiantly sing a song of Solomon.
With perfumed breath the sounds of night blow dreamily,
then fade away before the blast of dawn revives anew.
The call of hunting quickens and gives courage to the blood,
a rich, primeval voice of molten chorus in the sharpened air.
Then next, full blares the singeing braziers of a bitter war,
and charges, spurred and spattered to a glorious grave.
Till mournful, haunting mellowness soothes the spirit,
and pours contentment in a drowning lull of peace.

No.3 Woodwind

Gently, from lazy, summer oxbows adorned with pliant reeds,
the osiers whisper, mingling with gnarled, old willow's leaves.
A faintest breeze, by river's back-eddying, persuasive pull,
is channelled through green shoots to play the pipes of Pan.
Last trace of pale, sad morning's mist, sucked up by the sun,
sighing a watery greeting to the brightness of the day,
as night-time's shroud of dew sinks to the droning moss.
A sudden flight of urgent wings, down-feathering the air,
makes sallow rushes speak in rippling, high confusion,
and haughty poplars echo, shivering in a new-sprung wind.
New buds of sycamore sprout fingers from fat twigs,
that run and play along their neighbours in a jig.
The full-lipped gale blows bolder in mischievous snort,
as powdered catkins drop to drown in sparkling fleet.
The spirit of the forest, rude-wakened by the threatening storm,
calls out from hollowed, booming trunks to cease, be gone.
The sated silence also begs an audience to be heard,
as memory stirs in sleep, falters, and trembling, stills.

No.4 Percussion

Rhythms, as ancient as the pulse of man,
that measure and so keep time in check.
From galley's rows of oars dread speed,
to waltz of painted masquerade.
The deafening bells of peace and marriage feasts,
or sombre strokes declaring pestilence and plague.
Stretched skin's tattoo beats out the soldier's fear,
and snapping chestnut rattles high to proud-heeled boots.
Tambourines and May-cracked sticks of Morris,
the roll of distant thunder, or the scaffold's threat,
From hammered gongs and cymbals clash,
to ice-sharp hues of vibrant steel.
A myriad sounds of light and dark,
chameleon shades that blend and blur.
Bold flashes that widen the inner eye,
to delight and charm the ear.

The Village Organist

How many more will wend their way
around the old church path today?
Friend departing, or couple wed
baby christened, banns out-read?
Sunday-schooled, or first-confessioned,
Easter morn, Mayday processioned?
Carolled, at His birth remembered,
Harvest Festival Septembered?

So mused the village organist,
then thought of something that he'd missed.
Who'd play for him one future day
when in her coffin he would lay?
So many Sundays he had played,
in joyous descant often strayed.
Through bitter, winter snows he trudged,
and never missed, or much begrudged.

The springtime flowers fresh rejoiced
and summer's bounty gladly voiced.
At Autumn's gold he'd simply smile
as stained glass shone down on the aisle.
For Mother's Union he would play
and poppies-red Remembrance Day.
The great church rafters he had raised
and with the congregation, praised.

The old church organ was his friend
and many an hour would gladly spend
accompanying the stoic choir
at 'Sing-a-thons' to mend the spire.
The hymns and psalms he knew by heart,
"Trumpet Voluntary" from end to start,
Anthems, Handel's great "Messiah",
"Jesu, joy of man's desire".

Funeral dirged and Wedding marched,
through wind and rain and summer-parched.
He'd seen the vicars come and go,
and always they would want to know,
"Who is the village organist?
Does he any change resist?
Is he often ill, or no?
Is he 'High', or is he 'Low'?"

"How reassuring when one finds
an organist who never minds
how often, when, and what he plays
on Sundays, or those 'Special' days."
Oh, he just plays, and seldom frets,
and never in a panic gets.
For sixty years has played for free,
insulted if they mention 'fee'.

His fingers move upon the keys,
he just ignores the bellow's wheeze.
The well-thumbed pages, yellow-grey,
he hardly needs to find his way.
But the wedding dresses, pictures, flowers,
the 'video' and the threat of showers
are more important on 'The Day'
than what the organist will play.

But all the same, it would be dull
without the 'swell' or 'stops' at full.
'Flute' or 'Viola da Gamba',
'Vox Humana', 4 foot 'Tromba',
'Dulciana', 8-foot 'Bourdon',
16-foot Stopped 'Diapason'.
The pedals answer to his shoes,
his music echoes round the pews

The village organist is there
to play for rich, or poor, affair.
He plays them in, he plays them out,
is very rarely thought about.
But yet one day he will be missed
and then perhaps you will have wished
you'd listened what his fingers played,
now stiff and still and silent made.

Do not despair, he is not mute,
but plays a more celestial lute.
His fingers move behind some cloud
in music sweet, both soft and loud.
The village organist aspires
to play the tunes that God desires.
And, by the light of sun or moon,
just hopes the angels sing in tune!

The Performance

The animated conversation dies,
as stage lights breathe the platform into life.
A moment's pause, the side door pulls ajar,
tumultuous applause cuts like a knife.
A slight and dark-haired man walks calmly on,
smiles gently, bows, and sits with easy grace.
The audience quietens, clears its throat and waits,
stares tense, to watch his concentrated face.
His hands rise up, then fall like injured birds,
sweet notes sing out in perfect, measured time.
The sound of Bach flood through the famous hall,
pure elegance, an "*English Suite*" sublime.
Inspired, composed and written long ago,
that genius mind, through parchment, ink and quill.
By wood, taut wires, cast iron and ivory keys
this later *Maestro* links and pours his skill.
Through *Prelude, Allemande, Courante* he soars,
the nightingales, in envy, hold their breath.
Then *Sarabande, Gavotte, and Gigue* ride clouds,
as jealous larks wish silently for death.
The glorious music ends, our ears replete,
a thousand hands fly up and fill the air.
Appreciate in awe, complete delight,
this virtuoso's talents thrilled to share.
The mood then changed to passionate intrigue
in Chopin's great *Sonata, number three.*
Allegro maestoso soared up in joy,
Scherzo: molto vivace, hovering, free.
The gentle *Largo* glided calm, serene,
and wistful, like a frozen porcelain dove.
Then blazed *Finale: presto non tanto,*
a Phoenix rose in ecstasy of love.
The audience erupts in rapturous praise,
a treasured memory held for evermore.
The concert pianist bows and then retires,
brought back again, again, *Encore! Encore!*
Now silently remembering with my pen,
I think on words that William Congreve wrote,
"Musick has Charms to soothe a savage Breast,"
"To soften Rocks, and bend a knotted Oak."

- *Observation and Contemplation* -

My Shoes

Two.
Left and right.
Conceived at the same time.
Created, grown, and fashioned twins.
Lying together, joined by parental leather
of the same skin, linked, though not quite Siamese.

Un-boxed, their umbilical cords tied for the first time,
They tried out their first unsure, questioning steps.
I cared for them, and showed them off with pride.
Comforted them when they had training scrapes,
Pinched, squeezed, and got to know each other.
New recruits, on parade, ready for action, platooned.

Many a time they put me on and took me out,
I only adopted them for a while, my foster feet.
And then, when we were worn in and fitted so well,
We went miles together, like three musketeers.
We arrived at so many crossroads, and tossed a coin.
Oh, the places we went, I could write a book!

I mended them when they got old and leaked,
Two old men with old men's problems.
Shabby, down at heel, with thin soles.
I had them mended again, one last time,
As they had begun to lose their way occasionally,
In the Alzheimer time of their life.

And when they were no longer fit enough to march,
I pensioned them off, in retirement, with honours.
Taken off, they now lie helpless, but still together.
Occasionally I see them, at the back of my wardrobe
And we smile at each other, and nod, like old friends.
Remembering the miles…left…right…left…right.

My two old soldiers,
Paraplegic,
Proud.

69

Birthday

Your eyes look not upon this special place,
where once with mine they widened in delight.
As April spreads her white and pink and blue,
wild garlic, campion and forget-me-not.
One swallow darts above the sunset's gleam
and clouds of gnats, mad-jigging, mark the spot.
Young years roll back in memory very dear.
I know you will not mind me living-on my life.

A Welshman

How often have I sought your company,
to talk of this or that in friendship's mould.
Enlightened, or amused, confiding free,
your earnest wisdom, measured wit, unfold.

The staunchest ally man could ever meet,
no helping hand as ready, or so great.
Played the game, be that loss or victory sweet.
faced down the foe, integrity complete.

The bravest and the kindest heart to all,
his dearest ones no need to testify.
Bold, true and loyal, firm and fair his call,
that quiet strength, which he could justify.

So gaze on God, and wait awhile in rest,
sleep well, old friend, you're counted with the best.

Onion

A row of onions in my father's garden.
The green and brown of it all.
The growing and the dying.
Pulled , lifted, thrown away
and planted in the season's roundness.
The gnarled fingers I look on now were his,
the beetling brows, at when I dug too deeply for him,
and the faint smile around his lips as,
later on, I spaced them right,
now haunt me in the greenhouse glass.
These plants, like me, grew slowly,
I was impatient to see the hidden things below,
and tried to make the season happen quicker.
Easter preparation and Summer rain were all too slow
in bringing round the plump and praise of Harvest Festival.

And now I hold an onion in my hand.
The skins of time in wrinkling, crisping sere.
Smelling of my father's jacket, warm and safe,
a world concealed inside its heavy cloth.
The years peel off so easily, for a while,
then cling a little tighter as each layer
becomes more stubborn in its yielding.
The deadened brown becomes a greener shade,
the quick of life takes on a fresh appeal.
My fingers feel the slip of lighter, creamy sap
that floods my memory's keening joy.
Yet baulks the sharing of its inner self
in awkward, youthful blush of inexperience.

I take the knife, and cut,
its centre, infant life reveal.
A white and innocence laid bare
at the sluicing crunch against my nails,
The old, familiar strength assails my nose,
and stings my eyes, anticipates my mind to sense
the moist, crisp, succulence of earth.

These broken rings of time now viewed in curiosity,
the zest of life communioned on my tongue,
at this, the core of memory's thoughts,
in one small globe of pain,
no sweeter thing reminds me more.

71

Hannibal, on meeting Clarice

I stare in silence through bright bars of steel,
an evil, wicked monster, so I'm told,
with hideous mask. Kept dim, observed with zeal
in concrete tomb. Repulsive, buried, cold.

Hello Clarice, you've come to delve my mind?
To ask of me a favour? Read my eyes
intelligence? The tangled strings unwind?
Please do not bore me, that I would despise.

You must give back to me some hope, that I
may teach you how to think, and cunning be.
Take me away with you in your mind's eye.
Hide me under your skin, escape with me.

In love, we'll join, *flagrante delicti*,
Dine alone on liver and Chianti.

Sleep eludes him

And shall my mind to quietness and bland,
that plane serene, when sleep drifts numbly in?
Will consciousness let slip its damning hand,
in acquiescence of some calm within?

Mock tortures of a guilty kind prevail,
to scrape the tender vestiges full sore.
Alarms in brash battalions rend and wail,
a wrenched disharmony assaults the core.

One theme still reaffirms the trouble's worth,
and keeps that sluggard, carelessness, awake.
A conscience, troubled, relegates all mirth,
in knowing dusk comes long before daybreak.

So might I crave a peaceful mind, in sleep,
than counting sorrows, worries, debts and sheep.

Tsunami

Just a word.
A simple, terrifying word.
When you say it
it pounds through your head,
and wrings your heart.
That such a beautiful sounding word could bring such horror.
Those hypnotic images beamed worldwide
in sickening raw reality.
Watching the relentless sweeping away
of civilisation's small struggle.
Witness generations scattered like so much worthless dross,
and stare in numb and impotent fascination
on the cruel flotsam of a geographic phenomenon.

Our vast orb jolts and settles to a new shape,
a shape of blind indifference.
Deep, deep the old earth's indigestion rumbled
and belched destruction.
Explained and understood as a natural disaster,
yet beyond understanding in its viciousness.
A hideous natural unnaturalness.
This hopeless, helpless time suspends belief.
Yet still we believe in the frantic will to live,
to help, to heal, to carry on and accept,
and to let go and wake to another dawn.
Even after all this.

And after the inexorable surges
and after the dragging down
and the obliteration,
yet still, life remains.
Yet still hope transfixes
and man begins again.

Oh be afraid,
be very afraid.
And let death remind you of your life,
and concentrate your frailty to cling to hope.
And live for those that also lived.

Blue veins

Blue veins seeping through wedges of cheese,
        infecting the whiteness in tasteful disease.

Blue veins slick-snaking the valley's floor,
        from springs, to oxbows, estuary, shore.

Blue veins leeching from ore-laden rocks,
        then smelted to copper for high weather–cocks.

Blue veins ghosting the face of the moon
        in craters, reflecting the grin of a loon.

Blue veins in marble, statues of Rome,
        Corinthian colonnades lifting a dome.

Blue veins staining the old church spire,
        calmly conducting the lightning's fire.

Blue veins running from sorrowing eyes,
        behind darkened glasses of widow's disguise.

Blue veins shimmering clear winter nights
        kaleidoscope magic of Northern Lights.

Blue veins that flow from King Louis's head,
        which Madame Guillotine shamed into red.

Blue veins raised up on hands of the old,
        knotted, and knitting to keep out the cold.

Blue veins on paper, fading away,
        old poems recording the years of their day.

Alone in a crowd

All at once I saw you,
alone in the midst of a crowd.
They didn't see you,
for they were too close,
for the crowd only sees what is there.

You were not there, though your form was there,
but you were away from your form.
You smiled and turned,
this way and that,
as if you didn't care.

And the crowd just listened
to what you said,
listened, but heard not a word.
Your eyes were dead, their light was gone,
as you blinked and looked through the air.

The crowd looked back,
looked back and smiled,
turning this way and that.
Yet they were blind
to your watching stare.

But I watched, and I saw,
looking in from the edge.
Watching you blindly stare
through the crowd
through the air.

Alone in a crowd,
for the you, wasn't there,
and your heart
was as dead
as your stare.

Who did you think
was looking at you?
Did you
sense me
in the air?

The Picture

Oblong framing, gilded edges
floating, quiet string suspended.
Wide-cut mount of creamy colour
draws the eye to view intended.
These the bones, my picture hanging,
skin of glass to see the spirits
captured by the artist's working
through her palette's subtle limits.
Empty landscape makes excuses,
not including flowers blushes.
Bird-less, tree-less, only features
those of ancient hills and rushes.
Mounds in gloomy introspection,
brooding clouds, with sorrow ladened.
Chill the air, grey mist half-rising,
ominous, no house enlivened.
Where am I in this my picture?
No reflection in the distance?
Where the other men and women?
Hands that shake in warm acquaintance?
Nothing makes my scene more dreaded
than this one of hollow beauty.
Record of an empty moment,
born from pain or sense of duty?
I will step into this wasteland,
make my home behind the glazing.
Looking back from far perspective,
view the picture from the painting.

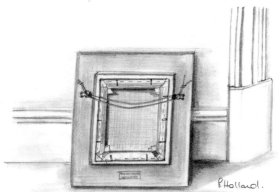

76

People in the park

Walking back home
through the park
I look at
them

An old lady pulling
at her shopping
bags small
gravity

The young man texting
unaware of my eyes
reading his
mood

Bread-throwing children
being dragged back
from the water's
edge

The gardener putting in
the colourless husks
to lie in
wait

One half of a hopeless
marriage with cheap
sherry on her
breath

Hand-holding couple walk
smiling to the bench,
putting down their
sticks

Laughing and shouting
boys speed past and
throw their
gum

High heels click by and
devotedly track the
silent bubbled
pram

The painful well-worn
jacket that left his
mates at
Dunkirk.

Resigned loving patience
to the girl with
the vacant
look

Perhaps they do not
know me at all
except in the
park

Prisoner

I look at your face
and ask you a silent question.
Without answering
you tell me what I need to know.

Sometimes when I look at you I feel sad,
and yet in your prison of steel
it is you who must know what sadness is.
Your hands hiding your face,
forever on your treadmill.

I keep the key that unlocks
your numbered cell.
Marking out your sentence,
certain of no release,
Uncompromisingly doing time
in the monotony of your life.

What are you thinking about,
reciprocating, contemplating, cogitating one?
The times we share are all too quick,
yet you can make my sadness seem even longer.

I am lost without you.
I cannot do without
your complicated style.
I am defenceless
to your mocking wit
.
You pull at my arm
and tell me to hurry.
I am always behind your quickness.

Even when I have you in my grasp,
you spirit slips away
like shattered quicksilver.
Can I never catch you up?

P Holland.

Even as I hold you
and stop you running away,
even then you laugh at me.
We depend on each other,
you and I.

Yet when I release you and sleep,
you still keep a vigil beside me
in the quiet time of the night

Though I control you,
my action giving you life,

Your spirit controls me,
your action ekes out my life.

What will you keep of me?

What will you keep of me, when I am gone?
What photograph, or book, or thing of mine?
My smile, or frown, of what we talked, or none?
What might remind you of my form, or time?

And which of those would give you peace of mind
to see, or hear, or know, and ease your pain?
When looking in my life, perhaps you'll find
a small and treasured piece you will retain?

Dear one, you will not need to search for me
in boxes, drawers, or frames of glass, or art.
Just close your eyes, and pause, and you will see
that I'm still with you, there inside your heart.

And what you keep of me, I know for sure,
is what I keep of you, for evermore.

Whose?

Whose eyes first looked and saw you
coming through the dawn,
saw the mist surround you
in the glory of your morn?

Whose eyes then always softened,
watched your sleeping form,
soothed in calm protection
from the threatening of the storm?

Whose eyes were guarded for you,
comforting your pain,
quiet in the sunset,
or sheltering from the rain?

Whose eyes have wept to see you
mix with rogues and fools,
then helped you start again
with a different set of rules?

Whose eyes have smiled upon you
when your sky was bright,
or ill, sad and weeping,
sat beside you through the night?

Whose eyes then hoped to see you
never bend or break,
strive, and be contented,
equal measure give and take?

Whose eyes may never see you
grey from life's attack?
Your mother's eyes will see you,
in the mirror, looking back.

Lux Perpetuum

There are those who can see,
yet are blind to the truth.

Some have reason,
but choose not to use it.

Others listen to what they want to hear,
especially about themselves.

Most will eat with you,
if they neither prepare, nor pay.

Many will give advice,
few will help readily.

Sympathy flows easily,
but dries up soon after it is poured.

An honest and simple answer
deserves the correct question.

A promise given and forgotten,
is a remembered disappointment.

Better a small gift simply given,
than generosity tied up with strings.

An opinion expressed professionally
may have value, but will certainly cost.

Treat all mankind the same,
your friends expect no more.

Confound your enemies with a smile.
Losing is the sole reminder of having.

Speak less, hear more.
Love all.

Listings

The things I love most are people,
though some I no longer see.
Unless I look inside my heart, and there they are for me.

Except when I climbed the church's steeple,
mainly the things that terrify me
are inside my head, so don't really exist too literally.

The things I wish I'd done, like gliding,
but then I can't stand heights, you see,
anyway, what's the point, now I'm too old to climb a tree.

All the places that made me anxious,
like the first time I swam in the sea,
or my first school party, when a girl came and sat on my knee.

All the places that I love to see
are those where I have the key.
Memories take me again and again, and I always go there for free.

All the beautiful things I've seen,
paintings, and statues, and topiary,
and playing a shiny new Steinway's black and ivory.

All the squalid places I've been,
Cairo, Colombo, Mombassa, Torquay,
where a drunk staggered home, and then stopped for a pee.

Memories and wishes and drinking tea,
Gliding and parties and climbing a tree,
Paintings and children that swim in the sea.

People and places, beggars, Tralee,
steeples and kissing and topiary,
marble and music, and you and me.

All inside
one head?
Dear me!

Daemon

Through the grey gloom, half-day, half-night,
where bitterest wind steals all away,
and cold is deathliest intent,
he journeys, ..agonized, ...alone.
A shattered soul that spins, degenerate in purpose,
to meet his fateful nemesis.

Not even leviathans venture here, no wolf, bear,
nor any thing that Nature gives a glimmering of life.
Immutable ice, yet further ice, carries his haunting quest,
beyond...away... resolved in singular rejection.

That other mind that reasoned, formed, gave life,
and then repulsed in answer, now is dead,
deep in the grounded sea.
Compassion, soured to loathing and regret,
an action unforgiving,
rues the day.

In anguished plea the Daemon yearned,
sealed with horror's threat,
a balancing request, and was denied, revoked,
foul-judged...maligned... and spurned.

And yet he was not blinded to the higher grace,
the nurturing milk of contact, the mirroring look of love.

The stolen fire once thrust into his heart, not asked,
is now an ash of hate and vile revenge.
Yet still he drives his hell on earth, a living death,
in dreaded wastes and furies desolation.

He howls an unimaginable howl of uttermost despair,
and welds his manacles of pain to hardened, galled profundity.
Then, to the storms that roar about his hideous form,
defiantly requests an end that even they will not allow.

And, fixed at last, abhorrent of a deathless life,
embalms in frozen fire, ...self-sacrificed.

Henry by Holbein

He stands, immovable,
ready to savour all that life can offer.
Arrayed in gold and silver thread,
wealth secular, or sacred, easy in the pickings,
speaks of his grasping envy.
The slashes, squeezing from the cloth
in fashionable cut, like scarlet wounds.
Like blood of those that incurred displeasure,
and feigned regret for their traitorous, small deed.

His feet firmer than any oak,
and yet, none lighter in the dance.

His arms, much widened,
eager to raise a sword, or racquet,
or crush the tenderest flower of his court.

His hands, gifted in the music,
could check the reins of strongest stallion,
weigh the purse, release the power, buy the ink
to write off any priggishness from Rome.

His girth speaks of his greed,
Fat fingers, ringed and double-ringed,
closed on the jewelled baselard.

His body, strongly male, so very male,
the jutting codpiece, overstating.
Symbolic of his proud virility,
and the downfall of his cankered, fruiting years.

His face, square, butchersome, and cruel,
set with eyes of selfish vaingloriousness.
Yet such soft mouth, that almost strays more to feminine,
in spite of the desire to impress.

He is a spoiled and pandered child of his own making.
He reigns, leaves none in doubt that he must be obeyed.
Yea, He is a royal beast, heraldic,
a lion, bull, hound, and unicorn.

But his eyes belie the spirit, the artist
holds the upper hand, a mirror to the soul.

Sad, this puppet of the years, to be brought down
by the splendour of his own conceit.

The dagger gives yet more away,
cuts the thread of awe in peevish honesty,
the soft underbelly of indulged excess, and also fear.

He is a King, full-dressed, a Majesty
commanding all within his gaze.

Yet the painter persuades me
to see the monster.

Grandma Pat's conversation with Harrison, 3 ½.

"Grandma, come and look at our Christmas tree!"
His eyes wide-bright and tugging hands,
the puppy innocence, with urgent words
of lisped exasperation, infected his child's plea.

"Grandma, Grandma, come quick and see the tree!"
Interrupting adult's boring conversation,
newly started, an unexpected visitation,
to share his bursting wonder at her knee.

"Grandma, Grandma, Grandma, see our tree!"
So she allowed his monumental effort,
forward steps, encouraged smiles of comfort,
delighting in his half a year and three.

"Grandma, Grandma, this is my favourite on the tree!"
taking off a cherub, so very carefully,
and held it in his chubby fingers tenderly,
waiting while she bent her head to see.

She took it slowly from his cradling palms,
said "It's lovely!", returned it to his reverential knack.
He answered, more potently than carols, hymns or psalms,
"Grandma, it's a baby with a butterfly on its back."

Wave

I read that you waved.
You looked through the panes,
through a small child's eyes,
alone, you waved.

I saw where you waved.
You looked at the world.
The world turned its back,
waved you away.

I heard that you died,
but you weren't alone.
Unable to wave,
able to die.

I hope, now, you wave
from a different place.
Where the world waves back,
and you can smile.

I think of your pain.
I think of your wave.
I think of your smile.
I think of your name.

A three year old child; abused, battered, tortured, burned with cigarettes, and murdered by the mother's drug-crazed lover. The mother was on drugs too, and, it appeared, was incapable of stopping what was happening. There was the suggestion she may have also taken part in ill-treating her child. The child was occasionally seen, shyly waving, from a second story window at passers-by in the street. During the investigation it seems that very few ever waved back at her. Local people heard the pitiful cries of the child, but no-one took the trouble to report it. No-one had ever seen the child outside the house. The media reported the case.

Stones

Consider the stones;
twisted into harsh rope,
threading the mountains of China,
keeping Emperors safe from the hordes
for a while.
Obsolete, tourist-trod and seen by satellite.

Ponder the stones;
hewn as a sullen feat,
linking two seas of Britannia,
keeping legions safe from the clans
for a while.
Superfluous, car-traversed and seen as preservation

Contemplate the stones;
raised in grim barrier,
negating the Berliner's choice,
keeping State safe from Democracy
for a while.
Dismantled, souvenir-sold and seen in scarred minds.

Discuss the stones;
drawn as a fresh line,
shifting occasionally in the sand,
keeping Arab away from Jew, God away from Allah
for a while.
Erected, hate-mortared and seen as constructive

See the stones;
fashioned by the hands of men,
formed, heaved, pressed, and willed.
Good fences make good neighbours don't they?
for a while.
Planned, concrete-set and seen as necessary.

Consider the stones;
grinding years,
marking graves,
quarried, waiting
for a while.
Petrified.

Comparison   *after reading Louis Untermeyer's "Portrait of a Machine"*

O perfect machine!
How the sculptor envies you;
His work a static, bloodless thing, stiff,
embittered, cold, sleeping the sleep of the dead.
How he must be jealous, unfulfilled,
to view your mass of pulsing, raw vitality,
your unashamed and noble, naked chassis.
Be awed by iron muscles with their piping veins,
your rods and pistons living, knowing things.
Feel your vibrant heat and smell your sweating oil,
and listen to the hum and sing of spinning cogs.
See the soothing grease and glorious plume of steam.
Compare, O Man of Old Renaissance, this new
Bold Fruit of Mind's Imagining and Form!
His white Carrara stands so pale and blind, no heart,
A dead, immobile mineral indulgence.
Discarded chips of hard, white, gorgon stone
Reveals a stark and vaunted, vain, heroic stance, unknown.
How long he chipped and scraped and carved,
and all for what? Some petty, false, polite acclaim?
Acknowledged admiration of his time, ill-spent,
displayed on barren, boasting plinth, exhibited, embalmed.

Oh no! A thousand-fold times no.
Machine, give me your life and metalled will!
Lend me your energy inspired!
Show me exuberant spans of joy
and thrill me with your steel accord!
From plan, made good the bold idea,
designed, and lathed, assembled, fired!
Kinetic spirit, tireless slave,
You move at my command!
In moving spheres of grinding force,
enmeshed and forged, relentless power,
subliminal in strength, resolved,
all eager for supreme desire:
The Will To Serve.

His mawkish statue; cover up in shame,
Lewd, still-born, illegitimate.
Machine; you breathe in motion's art,
My child, colossal, and alive!

War Boys

Entrenched, exhausted,
their end yet to come.
Living clay in no man's land,
with blood-shot eyes that stared.

Un-ripened fruit, foul-blasted in perpetual storm,
bleeding their juices, pressed back into their roots.
Their mad, un-natural landscape twisted, torn and wired,
embroiled with iron, and fire, and gas.

What hope, this lunacy? What future?
What lessons still remembered, or forgotten?
Boys become men,
and always make the same mistakes.

Take off their issued boots that brought destruction,
Take away their managed guns.
Bury them in their innocence,
and taste the guilt.

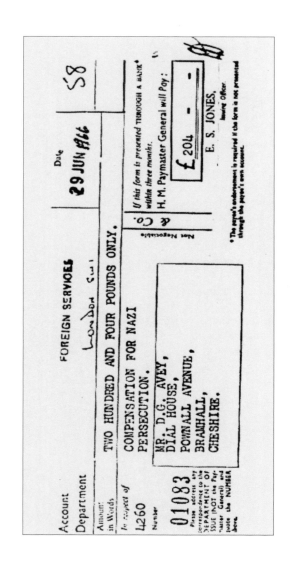

(Mr Avey no longer lives at Dial House, Bramhall, Cheshire)

90

"Stone walls do not a prison make, nor iron bars a cage"
Richard Lovelace 1618 -1657

(A mantra used by Mr. Denis Avey, a British P.O.W. .
He was captured twice, escaped twice, was wounded and captured a third time.
He was then imprisoned in, lived through, and survived Auschwitz.)

Receipt

Now he returns for us.
His memories; atrocities, slavery, hunger, cold, stench
and determination.
We try to be there with him, and fail.
You would have to be there to know.

We ask if it is possible to feel love or hate for the perpetrators.
He answers, without malice; indifference.

Years later he was sent a cheque, for the suffering;
Two hundred and four pounds.
He returned it.
They sent him a receipt.

Later, he was sent another cheque, for the suffering;
Thirty-one pounds.
He returned that also.
They sent him another receipt.

Then he returned his medals.
They sent a receipt.

He has never returned to that place,
yet a part of him could never leave.
It is always there.
You can't get a receipt for something you can't return.

We listened to his scars,
humbled we had not felt their pain.

Hannibal, before the Battle of Trasimene

From out my tent I see the Tiber's city stand,
so near, so far, the quest my father bade me sware,
When but nine years, in ancient Carthaginian land,
"Avenge the fallen, do or die!" thus spake he there.

Now sound the trumpet's shrill advance to Nubian men,
and elephantine echoes back resounding blast.
Recalling when they scaled the icy peaks again,
as now with sword unsheathed, spear poised, and shield held fast.

'Tis time to mount my chafing steed and, fearless, lead
this small, but loyal, potent force that none do quake.
Though out-numbered, on Legion's blood our steel shall feed,
'till all are vanquished, drowned in Trasimene's lake.

I vow to never speak the coward's word, retreat,
so bring me mountains, floods, and Romans to defeat!

on the death of the first British female soldier in Iraq

Warrior

No Amazon, she, but Boadicea.
Birthing freedom, scorning fear.

Armed with courage, honour, life.
This daughter, sister, mother, wife.

Stand still, reflect, no ill respect.
A warrior, gone, surpassed by none.

Ashes

They lifted him onto their shoulders,
holding him, gently.
Gaunt-grey stone rang back the bells,
and a pallid sun glowed
on the white, white flowers
of one small wreath,
Moving forward, inexorable as angels,
they laid him on the bier, ready.
Crimson curtains slid the last farewells,
and a hollow tape played
the sad lament of a twice
unchosen life.

They hoisted her onto their shoulders,
gripping her roughly.
Death-black boots rang the stones,
and a rust-red smear flowed
on the white-washed walls
of one small grief.
Marching forward, automaton soldiers,
they tossed her on the cart, ready.
Blazing chambers gorged on her bones,
and through the grim, brick chimneys
the pungent ash rose
of a first,
unchosen death.

He lifted her up in his arms,
holding her, gently.
Soft-green grass was under their feet,
above, the high white-clouded sky
of a new love.
Running together, shoulder to shoulder,
they played, as lovers, ready.
They talked of Christmas and Yom Kippur,
one Gentile, the other, Jew.
Once he gave her flowers.
But when she went,
he knew.

Holocaust poem: The present - a long time ago - and a few days previously.
All concerning an imaginary German Protestant Soldier and a Polish Jewess.

93

Shy Mary

Oh Mary, my dear, would you talk for a while?
Oh no, John, for talking would me soon beguile.
But, dear, just our talking would not be a trial.
No, no, John, I fear I would let myself smile.

Oh Mary, my dear, if I kissed your lips sweet.
Oh no, John, for kissing is so indiscreet.
But, dear, just one kiss will make all life complete.
No, no, John, I think we had better not meet.

Oh Mary, my dear, I shall die by and by,
Oh, no, John, I beg you, will you tell me why?
But, dear, how much longer will you remain shy?
No, no, John, don't ask me to give a reply.

Oh Mary, my dear, all my patience is gone.
Oh no, John, your questions I'm pondering on.
But, dear, for an answer I need only one,
No, no, John, for no I've decided upon.

Oh Mary, my dear, I would like to be wed,
Oh yes, John, I've waited for that to be said.
But, dear, it is Lucy will lie in my bed,
Oh dear, John, I fear that my tears will be shed.

Oh Mary, my dear, if you only had said,
Oh no, John, for you have another instead.
But, dear, if you'd followed me where I once led,
Dear John, I shall love you until I am dead.

The Girl with Auburn Hair

(Written in broadest dialect of the Manifold Valley in the Staffordshire Moorlands)

'A tell ov a mayd frum th'village grayn,   *maid *green
Agnes Pickrin' wur 'er naym.
Born at a farm 'neyth an 'ill cow'd Shayn,   *called Sheen
An' 'oud gyet orbun 'air.   *she had

Oh shay wur fair, theer's none denay,   *she *there is *deny
But wildt an' free, non fancy.   *not
Yit th'uther wenches made 'er cray,   *cry
An' taysd abairt 'er 'air.   *teased

Th'yong men o' frum rind abairt,   *around about
Tray'dt the best fut win 'er.   *for to
B'shay wur chusy, wi'airt a dairt,   *doubt
An' stalldt 'em wi''er stare.   *stopped

A'th'village Wakes thay danced 'er rairnd,
'Er eyes wur o' a-sparklin',
Win lads exed tek 'er whum, 'er frairnd, *asked *home
An' shuke that orbun 'air.

Win Agnes grew ter womanhood,   *when
'Er Mother towd 'er then,
As shay wur born o' chance-childt blood, *an illegitimate
An' th'Feyther, none knew where.

Then th'uther wenches spiteful wur,
When it gyet airt ont' gossip,
Thay turndt the backs an' laughed at 'er
Sed, "Cut yer orbun 'air!"

Well, Agnes back t'th'farm 'er ran,
An' tayerful, sobbed an' crayed,   *tearful *cried
Shay exed 'er Mother "Wheer's the mon,
"Give mey this orbun 'air?"

'Er Mother's face then fell o' gray,
Shay bit 'er lip i'shame,
"A gypsy lad, wi' mey did lay,"
"An' 'ey 'ad orban 'air."

Agnes ran <u>airt</u> on t'th'ill,   *out
An' 'id among <u>o'</u> rocks.   *all
Shay 'eaved 'er 'eart wi' <u>scraitin'</u> still,   *crying
E'en th'<u>shape</u> were watchin' there.   *sheep

Er' lay theer thinkin' "What's ter cum?
"Who'll luke at mey frum nair?"
"<u>A'l 'orn it</u>, though, what's done is done,"   *I'll put up with it
 "Fer mey, ar nothin' care."

<u>Neyht</u> drew in, an'th'<u>moun</u> full rose,   *night *moon
Yit still 'er lingered theer,
Shay fell inter a <u>fritful</u> doze,   *fretful
An' dreemt o''er feyther's 'air

Well, darkness passed, an' dawn <u>cropt</u> in,   *crept
Shay wok up wi' a start.
'Er shivered wi' 'er frock sa thin,
An' damp 'er orbun 'air.

Then Agnes run frum offa th'ill,
Cross th'<u>pasters</u> dewy sward.   *pastures
Th'valley filldt wi' mist o' still,
A saight o' <u>beowty</u> rare.   *beauty

Shay crossed thro' th'edge, an' int't'lane,
Then stopped, surprised ter sey,
A yong mon, leading 'orse an' <u>wain,</u>   *cart
An' whistlin', wi'out a care.

"Na' then, lass, what's up?" 'ey axed,
"Tha lukes a bit upset,
<u>Wut'na</u> tell, ar't sad?, or <u>vexdt?</u>   *Won't you? *angry
Tha's gyet sich pretty 'air!"

Shay <u>gloppendt</u> wur, 'er body shuke,   *dumbstruck
'Ey 'eld 'er wi' 'is eyes,
An' neyther brok their knowin' luke,
Su silent, buth did stare.

'Ey <u>fexed</u> 'er kindly in 'is gaze,   *He fixed
An' waited till shay'd calmed,
"What's thi name?, wheer gu thi ways?,
<u>Swait</u> lass wi' orban 'air!"   *sweet

96

"Agnes Pickrin', frum Shayn 'ill,"
'Er answerdt, blushin' bright,
"Br'av gyet many troubles still,   *But I've
 A'm non abairt t'share."

Th'yong mon quickly took 'er 'and,
An' tender 'eld it theer,
"A trouble shared's a trouble banned,"
Ey sed, wi' voice o' care.

"Gyet they ont' cyart, a'l tek thi wum,   * home
Albert Holland, that's mi name.
Well o'er river's weer ah'm frum,   *where
On't Glutton side o' wair."   *(a village) *weir

'Ey tuke 'er back t'er mother's place,
An lifted 'er dine frum th'cyart,   *down
'Ey gazed inter 'er pretty face
An' stroked 'er orban 'air
.
"A'l cum an' sey thee, once i'a while,"
'Ey sed, "if tha dusna' mindt."   *don't
Shay niver spok, b'give a smile,
That niver smildt sa fair.

Thay courtdt all o'th'summers long,
As th' yong 'uns orlis do,   *always
Till at last, theer love sa strong,
A ring were blest to wear

Su Albert n'Agnes 'appily wed,   *So
Thay lived at 'Stannery',
O'er fifty yeer, wur their homestead,
The good an' bad to share.

I'mey, theer blood flows wharmly still,   *In me *their
Ah'm proud ter tell thee nair,   *I'm *now
Mi Great-Grandmother, off Shayn 'ill,   *my
That lass wi' orban 'air

97

The Ballad of William Billinge

In Longnor's churchyard is a grave,
where William Billinge lies.
His simple life was long and brave
yet strange, as none denies.

His tombstone there records his time.
both birth and death revere.
His battles waged in foreign clime
on sandstone slab writ clear.

Now William's birth, it can be told,
was in a cornfield near.
At harvest time, the season's gold,
there smiled his mother, dear.

His birthing-place was Fawfieldhead,
in Longnor's parish bounds,
In 1679, t'was said,
her infant first made sounds.

The country lad like willow grew,
as straight and bold and tall.
The village green his laughter knew
with friends and strangers all.

Then William got 'the call away',
to fight in campaigns grim,
For freedom, and the foes dismay,
in lands unknown to him.

So at the age of 23,
"King's Shilling," William took.
In service of His Majesty,
and under Sir George Rooke.

Some glory then he keenly sought,
now trained to go to war,
He helped to take Gibraltar's fort
In 1704.

In valiant form, God-fearing might,
he bravely fought and true.
Yet in his heart, he ne'er lost sight
of faith, that brought him through.

His next campaign was Ramillies,
Marlborough's battle-ground,
where William's 'Sword of Damocles',
was o'er him, hanging, found.

'Twas on that day, in fateful state,
when all seemed black, sighed he,
"Dear Lord of earth and heavens great,
my life, I offer Thee."

"Thou know'st today I'll busy be,
my actions I regret.
Watch o'er, and hear my honest plea,
do not Thou me forget."

The battle raged, and men fell dead,
the fighting was the worst.
As cannon roared, the sky rained lead,
and William thought him cursed.

At conflict's height, in deathly pall,
smoke-blackened was the sky,
A Frenchman's well-aimed musket ball
shot William in the thigh.

Then heaving heart swelled in his breast,
his eye did drop a tear,
"From East to West, home is the best."
he said to comrade near.

His friend spoke up, "Now Will, give cheer,
and halve this bread in two,
Although we have not meat or beer,
you cut, I'll choose, split true!"

"Plain bread we'll eat, and for our drink,
cold water from the spring.
We'll share our ration, swim or sink,
and make a feast, and sing!"

They drank and ate the simple fare
of fellowship's shared bread.
A bullet whistled through the air,
his comrade fell down dead.

A soldier's life can sudden end,
they know it so to be.
As William wept o'er his best friend,
he whispered "Sleep, you're free."

There's many a British soldier died
that lies in far-off land
Their honour cannot be denied
on hillside, plain or sand.

Though wounded, William rose again,
and to "Attention!" stood.
The day was won by Marlborough's men,
with Dutch, our allies good.

So Flanders and Brabant were freed
In 1706,
and 'Sun King' Louis's pompous greed,
was stopped, with all his tricks.

The French, though led by Villeroy,
defeated, to their cost,
from General to drummer-boy,
They 15,000 lost.

Though William campaigned far from home,
his luck was, he returned
to end his days on native loam,
a resting place he'd earned.

One day, in aged years, he went,
on glorious summer morn,
the cornfield's harvest imminent,
and saw where he was born.

His eyes filled up, his breath was caught,
he gazed with trembling heart,
and murmured gently, "Is there aught
surpasses God's great art?"

The pleasant cornfield's ploughed-up soil
was sown, with faith, not dread.
And harvested in golden toil,
From seed to grain to bread.

'Twas very odd, the same cornfield
where William first drew breath,
Now caught him as he fell, to yield,
in peaceful, painless death.

Not many men begin and end
their life in self-same field.
And in between those times defend
the right, the weak to shield.

The muffled drum, and sad 'Last Post',
in honour, they did play.
His life was long; its end had come,
in Longnor's earth he lay.

My tale is done, though be not sad,
like William, battle through.
Plough straight, fight well, and harvest glad,
your trust in God renew.

Aquae Arnemetiae

'The Waters of the Goddess of the Grove' - Buxton

In ancient times, within a vale, there rose a clear, warm spring,
and there a race, called heathen now, their Goddess gifts did bring,
From deep within the limestone hills those early tribes once knew,
with simple minds, but honest awe, they thanked her sacred dew.
By circled stones, from earthen pots, they took and drank their fill,
though once, at summer sun's eclipse, a terror gripped them still.
Then moon moved on and light returned, the waters never slowed,
this constant stream ne'er failed them once, all seasons round it flowed.

Then later came the sound of iron, and marching, sandaled feet,
the native men were soon enslaved and humbled in defeat.
New Roman road then reached the glade, and found its healing flood
by legions might the hallowed place was seized and stained with blood.
The conquerors built, in votive thanks, a fountain flowing free,
named *Aquae Arnemetiae*, from local deity.
A pleasant baths to wash and cure, at war and sport they strove,
in honoured, healing waters of the Goddess of the Grove.

Yet empire failed, as time rolled on, the Latin came and went,
the darker ages dawned, yet still the waters gushed unspent.
Then Vikings, Anglo-Saxons, Danes and Normans held the place,
as Christian monks and priests baptised, with water's simple grace.
So *Buckstones* was, by *St. Annes Welle*, a place where pilgrims came,
to quench their thirst, in faith to praise it's ever-growing fame.
The Queen of Scots, by Talbot held, on *Old Hall* windowpane,
etched diamond words, her health restored, yet freedom ne'er regain.

In Georgian times, a noble Duke, the fifth, of Devonshire,
proposed to raise the town, a mighty scheme his grand desire.
Great architect, John Carr of York, was called in to design
a curving palace, columned, arched, with balustrading fine.
The fashionable and gentlefolk all came from far and wide
to take the waters, dance and card, in lodgings to reside.
So Buxton's famous *Crescent* was a jewel to behold,
men spent their wealth to buy their health, spa water, liquid gold.

Industrial Revolution brought the train, the Age of Steam,
Victorian iron, glass colonnades, distilled from Paxton's dream.
More grand hotels, new public baths, and crystal concert hall,
The Dome, by Robert Rippon Duke, the masterpiece of all.
From stables to a hospital the building was assigned,
new hydropathic cures were found for ills of every kind.
The thermal water's healing powers employed in many ways;
immersion, douches, needle, vapours, massage, surge and sprays.

The Buxton Baths, with bracing air and pleasant hills around,
pavilions, fountains, gardens, sport and leisure all abound.
A skating rink, with curling stones, for frozen wintertime,
and *Opera House* for culture, by Frank Matcham's plan sublime.
The wealthy built fine houses and decided they would stay,
while charabancs brought tourists who came only for the day.
From candle's glow to gas lamps, now electric lights blazed bright,
and still the waters flowed in ever-constant, pure delight.

Again there came more troubled times, of darkness, fear and dread,
the gallant men were called to fight, and counted in the dead.
And twice the worldwide nations bled, in anguish shed their tears,
and twice the fires of war were quenched, and ploughshares made from spears.
As peace returned the changing times brought travelling by air,
exotic holidays abroad with all-inclusive fare.
So Buxton's popularity then faded for a while,
as tourist's curiosity explored a different style.

The closing twentieth century then revived the Spa town's fate,
a thirst for mineral water in its pure and natural state.
The Buxton Festival was born, a cultured treasure trove,
again the people flocked to drink the nectar of the grove.
The glory of Grand Opera, Plays, Lectures to impress,
a vibrant Fringe, Jazz, Cabaret, and also G & S.
The pagan spring of long ago is still with flowers dressed,
a custom born in Peakland hills, which clergymen have blessed.

Alas, the famous hospital beneath *The Dome* is gone,
now *Derby University*, for each and everyone.
Our town entrusts its future state to him that freely thinks.
the thirst for education from the fount of knowledge drinks,
The Crescent waits, in anxious state, in hope to wax again,
spa water is our treasure to conserve, and health retain.
So, pure and pleasant fountain, pray forever may you flow,
come quench your thirst, revive your life, with Buxton's H2O!

Youn 'af fert' flit

Ar niver did upon mar wurt!
Yo arner airt ter bid,
liggin' theer o' of a peece.
Youn ayther 'af fert' arter,
or ilse Youn 'af fert' flit!

Thees God gi'en daise,
Well shall thi waiste?
Win o'oth' hee is cut an' swotht,
wints teddin' airt tuth' braize,
An' dawn thar's yit fert' taiste.

Tha's bin airt o' nayhts
A'cortin' rairned abairt.
A slattern huckrel th'as fund thi'sen.
tha'll mek thi bed, an' lie thi dairn,
But non bi'us ar dairt!

'Appen tha's geyt er foaled 'ast?
Tha'll not be fust ort' last.
Win lads ar' men thi louws thur'sen,
an' trouble follers on.
Geyt thi up, an' fast!

Cum thi dairn tha mucky arse!
Th'daise aif gon fer thay.
Tha'll swet thi trouble airt i'th sun,
tho tha's up an' fired thi gun!
ilse flit thisen t'dee!.

Yar, mi lad, tha'll smart sum mower,
Win th'Justice co's thi shame.
Thi huckrel's dead,
I'th wurk-hise bed,
thi chance-childt's geyt thi name!

Wots this, mi lad, ay nay!
thart 'ingin 'igh by th'rope!
An' it's scraight ar must,
i'th heefayld's dust
Tha'rt dead, an' that's no 'ope.

Cum thi dairn, mi lad,
Th'art stiff all o'er, an' gree.
A'l kape thi chance-childt,
Cum what may,
Tha's flit, an' arl rue t'dee.

You'll have to go

Well I never, upon my word!
You're not out of bed,
lying there altogether.
You'll either have to alter
or else you'll have to go!

These God-given days
will you waste?
When all the hay is lying in rows,
wants *tedding** out to the breeze,
and dawn you haven't yet tasted.

You've been out at nights
courting round about.
You've found yourself a sluttish tart.
As you make your bed, you'll lie on it,
But not in my house I doubt

Perhaps you've got her pregnant?
You're not the first, or the last.
 Boys become men they lose themselves,
 and troubles follow.
 Get up, be quick about it!

Come down, you dirty arse!
The day's half gone for you
You'll sweat it out in the sun
Though you've got her pregnant,
Or else move out today!

Yes, my lad, you'll smart some more
When the Magistrate calls you to book.
Your tart's died
 in the workhouse,
 your bastard's got your name.

What's this, son...oh no!
You've gone and hung yourself!
Now weeping is all I will do
in the hayfield's dust
You're dead, and now there's no hope.

I'll cut you down,
 You're stiff and grey
 I'll keep your baby
 Whatever happens,
 You're gone, and I'll rue today.

Circa 1850: An old farmer angrily calls his ne'er-do-well son to get up. He knows that this son has got a girl into trouble, and has just found out she has died giving birth in the workhouse. He enters his son's bedroom to find that he has committed suicide.

105

Once

Once there was a new-born girl
with all her life before her.
Innocent as April showers,
her smiling parents' daughter.

Once there was a fair-haired girl
who played in the sun all day.
She saw fairies above the boughs,
in the pink and white of May.

Once there was a brown-haired girl
bare-foot by river in June.
She skipped through fields in cotton blouse,
and stared at the rising moon.

Once there was a black-haired girl
who would grow her wings and fly.
She tasted all that life allows,
moth to the flame of July.

Once there was red-haired girl
the height of silken fashion.
Unfaithful to her wealthy spouse,
in selfish August passion.

Once there was a grey-haired girl
with too much to remember.
Sat alone in her wheelchair drowse,
in cooling, sad September.

Once there was a white-haired girl
who lay in a narrow bed.
Beside, a vase of wilting flowers
from someone she thought was dead.

Sheep in Snow

The snow had blown to a desert of drifts,
and drowned the walls in new-filled graves of white.
The ghosts of snakes ran wild before the wind,
glistening the swell in icy wreaths of light.
Old wrecks of trees in half-mast sails of rime,
root-anchored still by hoar-scaled chains in spite.
The thickened hedge in spindrift half-submerged,
as greying dawn showed blizzard's cruel night.

With scarf of wool tied firm across my face,
warm-wet by breath, the outside stiff and cold,
Our hats pulled down and tight across our brows,
and doubled coats from prudent moth-years old.
Hard slap of leggings rhythm over boots,
in keen wind's nine-tailed lash of biting scold.
The three of us set off in anxious mood,
 to find, and bring the lost sheep back to fold.

We trudged, and swayed, and sank up to the hips,
with laboured steps, eyes screwed against the glare.
The landscape's altered form lay odd and new,
strange banks, fresh mounds that once were never there.
No birds in flight, all silenced by the storm,
dead tops of thistles quivering in thin air.
Old hollows filled, and outcrops hung in shrouds,
the land bled white, embalmed in haste, laid bare.

Then, overhead, grim clouds closed in once more,
in black battalions ominously cursed.
The spinning wind, with new threat, raised the game,
we staggered on, but feared the very worst.
New snow swept down in hideous, smothering mist,
old snow whirled up in gravity reversed.
The howling gale our sight and breath cut short,
white terror on us bitterly dispersed.

The three of us; my father, sister, me,
kept close for comfort, and for safety's sake.
With shovels, two, and stick to probe the drifts,
then paused by copse, as storm showed little break
We shouted to each other in the blast,
we must go on and save the lives at stake.
The slowly sinking bushes left behind,
our footsteps quickly filling in the wake,

With dragging limbs and shattered hopes in tow,
like castaways on crushing pack-ice floes,
We floated half-drowned, frozen and in dread.
while treading snow that gripped in furrowed throes.
Then, all at once, in front of us a barn,
abandoned, roofless, ruined and morose.
Stood stark, alone, and powdered like a wig.
a harbour yet, to shield the furies blows.

My father shouted, pointing to the walls,
in disbelief, yet knew of what he saw.
Where drifts, so deep the gable lay half-sunk,
showed holes that spoke of buried sheep for sure.
With new strength, inner-charged, we dug in haste,
our shovels baling out in frantic chore.
Then carefully, the breathing holes till last,
first one, then two, and finally the score.

The ewes, though weak, unsteady, all alive,
their fleeces clogged in balls of frozen snow,
stood close and panting, nostrils blowing steam,
their silent thanks we had no need to know.
The storm, now thwarted of it's evil claim,
retreated back, the shrieks in lessening flow.
We turned for home, and followed by the flock,
the spark of life burned hot in heartfelt glow.

As winds abated, flakes of white died down,
far moors rose through the mist, afloat, and calm.
While trees, close-furled and frosted-sugar-spun,
their rigging stiff as glass, were docked in balm.
Our voyage back with each step lighter grew,
till, finally we saw in front, the farm.
Our weary group, in sunset's lengthening light,
drew nearer to the homestead, safe from harm.

The rescued sheep now joined the larger flock,
all counted, fastened in, and fed with hay.
As shorter day gave in to nights long black,
then slowly rose the crescent's silver ray.
Old farmhouse kitchen's warm and savoury smells,
a prelude of the tastes to come, gave play.
All curtains drawn, the roaring log fire glowed,
the starlit sheep lay quiet, none astray.

Soliloquy

'Course, 'ays gone nair,	*Of course, he's gone now*
Bur' ah'm still 'ere.	*But I'm still here.*
'Ay went an' dun it,	*He went and did it,*
A'th'end oth'yeer.	*At the end of the year.*
Sixty-fower,	*Sixty-four,*
Naioo tyme at'o.	*No age at all,*
Thro th'war an' pace,	*Through the war and peace,*
Leafs ryse an' fo.	*Leaves rise and fall.*
We'en buth wurked 'ard,	*We'd both worked hard,*
Aye, an' 'ard it wur,	*Yes, and hard it was,*
I'th feyldt an'th'yard,	*In the fields and the farmyard*
Scruws? Fer shuer!	*Rheumatism? For sure!*
Naioo childer lef',	*No children left*
O gone awee.	*All gone away.*
Ah sit, beref',	*I sit, bereft,*
Anuther dee.	*Another day.*
'Ay'd 'ad enaioo,	*He'd had enough,*
'Ay'ad, be 'eck.	*He had, by heck.*
'Ay tuk up th'knife,	*He picked up the knife,*
An' slit 'is neck.	*And cut his throat.*
Suicyde's	*Suicide's*
A mortal sin,	*A mortal sin,*
Th'parson sez.	*The parson says.*
Naioo wings fr'im.	*No wings for him.*

The word 'no' *is pronounced as* '**n**', plus '**air**' plus '**oo**' = "**naioo**"
The same '*sound*' *is used for* '*enough*' – *'Eh'd 'ad* **enaioo** - *He'd had enough*

The Two Sprigs O' Heather

All over the Highlands, on mountains and moor
there grows a wild plant that the clans all adore.
The heather, rich purple, by glen, crag and tor,
but rare is white heather and lucky for sure.

The Laird of a castle was seeking a bride,
his bloodline was noble but had too much pride.
A rich merchant's dowry then made him decide,
the daughter obeyed, but she secretly cried.

The Laird's cloak was purple, his manner was bold,
he gave her white heather, though his heart was cold.
He laughed at the merchant, so feeble and old,
rode off with his daughter and all his fine gold.

The Laird and his Lady on soft, summer morn,
united in tartan and wedding dress worn.
The White and the Purple they danced until dawn,
then bedded on feather and wool newly-shorn

The Lady was sad, though a new-married wife,
the Laird was so cruel, which caused her much strife
Her face white with sorrow and lonely her life,
his anger all purple, his words like a knife.

This ill-married couple were parted by war,
the Laird left in armour, for glory or gore.
She stayed in his castle behind a barred door,
and stared through her window across to the moor.

In May time the Lady went out for a ride,
right over the moor where the young grouse abide.
She met with a gypsy, in him did confide,
by August, as lovers they lay side by side.

The two sprigs o' heather, one purple, one white,
they're found in the Highlands, a beautiful sight.
The white was a Lady, she was pure delight,
the purple, her gypsy, with eyes flashing bright.

The Laird then returned from his battles so brave
but found that the Lady had gone to her grave.
She'd left him a baby, his line for to save,
its father, the gypsy, was hung as a knave.

The baby was raised by the Laird as his own,
he needed an heir that would sit on his throne.
He knew that the boy by another was sown,
the secret was safe till the lad was full grown.

The son of the Lady was now in his prime
he learnt that the Laird hung a gypsy one time
With eyes flashing bright, on his horse he did climb.
revenge for his father was not before time,

The Laird, he was slain by his only male heir,
his head on a pole, for the ravens to share.
And now from the tower his sightless eyes glare
across to the heather forever to stare.

All over the glens and the highlands so fair
the purple and white have a memory to share.
The new Laird was born of the lover's affair
and two sprigs o' heather forever will wear.

Randomdragons

Dragon! Pucker to degenerate mild pyrosis in your hate!
Your unexpected holy terrors are your second-comings now,
perhaps to choose?

Overstayed in optive mood, you must miskick!
Or else I might, in temper, hold your throat.
Beware your lifelong servitude,
perhaps to lose?

Dragon! must all the slipping of your scales
deny what I have hoped to nullify?
You ask me in my sleeping dreams
to fulfil those finite intimations,
those pitter-patter drops that will not stop.
Dragon!....you fight!

But I can hold your self-pitied intercostals
in the twinkling of my eye.
Much as you will try, I cannot be bought.
So take back those random tortures, they are tamed!
Random!... you tried!

The writing's on the wall!
Mene, mene, tekel, upharsin.
Nebuchadnezzar has drunk his wine,
and I am tired.
Dragon!... be gone!

But wait,
no, stay a while,
perhaps we can achieve some pensose peace.
A friend can always criticise, and live.
Random!... you lie!

My steadfast weakness is my strength,
your strength your coming weakness.
Dragon!....you die!

The Four Humours Abstracted   *after reading Lucky's speech in "Waiting for Godot"*

You cannot abstract things, for they, if conceptualised as a thought,
       qua theory, concrete, is what we know by touching,
or, there by grouping colours and shapes, qua, prisms,
       and, although not things, you can envy them their reality.
I go green with jealousy, achieving it's effect by choler,
       more like a liverish yellow, qua, bile,
as recognised reality when you can't see it, is a humour
       that was once separated from something else.
An abstract of body, qua, phlegm or melancholy,
       not tangible or conditioned, when you can't comprehend, qua, it.
Melancholia pours, or appears as an expression,
       manifests itself in tears, evaporating to nothingness,
which does not appear as being there, qua, invisible,
       as not being concrete. Unless you can concretize it, qua, seen.
What is felt as physical black? Black is not a colour.
       Pigmentless reality, which I don't understand.
Why is so much theorized rather than practised?
       Nothing is, that which cannot be, if thought about,
or disseminated by mind over matter.
       According to an idea which disengages fact,
and which you have to know about, not think,
       when you cannot see it, qua, what is in front of your eyes.
Although you can produce abstract painting,
       it isn't there, apart from in the head, or eyes,
only seeing or feeling that which, concretely, is.
       To be known as a physical interpretation,
not felt like an emotion, am I jealous of abstract?
       Because, metaphysically, who cannot see black?
Even though it is, or isn't, conceptualised.
       It could be abstractedly visualized, qua, sanguinity.
Are we are envious of this thing? Bloodless,
       or un-thing, physiologically manifested, if obscure,
which isn't there? A colourless void, qua, vacuum.
       Unreality, aka Abstract, qua, amorphous condition,
is when the idea of some phlegmatic thing,
       to be or not to be, is formed cerebrally, in the mind's eye..
It only becomes concrete, as and where, it will.
       By nature's summarization: the black nothingness
of its humours, or concretized by, qua, concept,
       preferring sanguinity, qua, blood, life, or that
imponderable which cannot be actualised in form.
       Humours abstracted;
black, green, yellow, red.
       A difficult rainbow.

Abracadabra (Eunoia)

Alas! Cassandra always asks alms at a Casablancan Alhambra and that pays a Panama
barman at Samarkand. That alarms all fans at a Kabbalah rally, (mascara awash and
kaftan craft). Sarah Macallan can add awkward anagrams at Mad Sam Adam's bazaar.
Zsa-Zsa sways a samba as a crass man falls athwart palms, crawls back at last past a
jacaranda jar, rants and stamps a standard haka. Dawn warns Barrabas at Caracas. That
may appall all Mama Cass fans that can crash ash at an Alabama mantra rant. Grandma
snaps and slaps a hand-bag snatch man. Da-da as Art a la ga-ga. Alan Ladd stalks and
bags Madam Bacall, That's karma! Hagar starts a war and tanks attack a Saharan
caravan, as an adamant Ack-Ack blasts blanks all day and masks a backward task. A
last stand at Ramada barracks (all crash, thrash and gas-masks) starts talks at Amman.
Anwar Hassan falls, bawls, and has bad scars. Shah Adnan Khan brawls,
grabs land at Ararat, and calls talks. A task and a half that can call a pact that lasts.
"Jaw-Jaw Stalls War-War!" "Haw-Haw Calls!" "Japan Falls." Hash stash attracts a
crass class that lacks cash as banks crash. Call a man a cad that plays craps (aghast at a
bad hand, flaps, and has a catnap at a cat flap.) Hard, dank marram grass wants a part as
half all calabash skank tabac. Draw a drag, gag and gasp, and grasp at an ash tray.
Ashraf nags a man that had a Grappa flask, sways and falls, calls a cab, trawls a car
crawl and catcalls call-gals. Manhattan Rastas rap ratta-tat-tat. Sharks trawl and stalk
sprats as prawns spawn. Crabs grab at a ray as a Catalan catamaran's flag sags at half-
mast, snags and snaps. All hands snatch at a flat hatch catch as snappers swap sprats.
Mark Nall has smart Art marks at Harvard that Alan Hall can't match at all, and that's a
fact! Can't an Alaskan lass Can-Can? A Kansas gal can! Bach's harp plays flats and
sharps, snaps, and falls apart! A raw jackdaw flaps away. Dawn swans thrash a lazy
carp, and that thwarts a alpaca that has a warm Astrakhan hat. Amy plays a
Madagascan cantata a la Palma calmata. Panama hats hang awkwardly anyway!
Malacca maracas manyana? Papa pawns paw-paws and papayas. Pam plays a small
part as Satan, all dark sarcasm at an arty-farty Plaza play. Carla at La Scala has an away
day at Salamanca. Alas!, can Allah call afar that all calm hands salaam Balaam?
Alack!, Galahad bawls that all Allah's Arab bands can't ban all psalms, (a bad path that
galls), and grants Valhalla a vast gala that shall attract all. Hark!, hark!, a lark! Halal
Shaman calls "Allah Akbar", (rants   and cants) and warns all Arab lads away that want
a bad lass at a camp vamp party. That can attract scant Prada pants, pack a slack brash
bra and lack a yashmak). Catch a rash? Stay away! Grab a mat, fall flat and pray! At
Ramadan, can Allah say any man's small parts (aka banana) want a fatwah? A
bandsman bans any gray bandanas at grand bandstands and plays Trad Jazz, an
Arkansas march, Black Sabbath, Bart and Baccarat. "Daft bastard!" calls a mad Jack
Tar, a small brawn, as a bad yachtsman yaws all gallants and stalls a tall craft. Avast all
hands! Hard rattan mats and pampas grass lawns lack that brash glass razzamatazz (and
that attracts Fat-cat ass!) Manx cats can catch rats that tabby cats can't. Canary Wharf
flats always attract Stars that carry all cash-back cards. Has any Madam a hand-bag that
has a brag tag? That's A-class Ad Astra! Aardvarks drag a pathway that ants want as a

114

damp kraal camp crawl. A ram and a lamb walk a day and a half and stay at a farm that has tall grass and a warm barn. A small hawk calls and alarms a rat as a vast wasp swarm attacks a ram's flanks. Sandra has angst, as a damn drama class starts at Gstaad and crafty staff clash. What starts as a mass mantra rant at a Jazz cabal has a last waltz schmaltz. Grads lack tact, anarchy starts, and bad cads ransack a Rasta pasta stash. Black lads saw planks at damp swamp shacks and attack back at last! Japan has damp sampans and Lapland bans all bland jam pans. Swatch watch? Bad batch! Brash trash that straps cash. Tarmacadam has a matt black plan at a Clackmannan plant. Tall straw walls fall, warts and all. Scamps plan plasma scam. Tramps walk all day, may fall at a bad cramp attack, lack a wash, a gamp and a warm camp. Man-traps can catch tramps, as tank traps can trap tanks. Anna bans all Trabant cars as Barry's Packard charabanc stalls badly at a Mazda rally. Scary hawks scan, harry snatch-and-grab, and carry away a sad lark's March hatch. Grand chaps ban a bad, camp man that black-balls a hard-hat grant. Abanarzzah has a taramasalata, cassata and kalamata salad, ananas and a flat Tartar banana. Harry, what a bad lad, has a black flat cap, and can stand far back, cast at a faraway char that snaps a gnat at a canal path bank.

Cha-cha-cha, Ma-ma, what a party!

Thanks, Frank and Sally.

Ta-ra-aa-aa-aa

Things I heard today

Well, hang on, you never reminded me.
But you wouldn't have cared anyhow.
Did you tell him to come at half-past three?
Yes, but that's not what started the row.

Better for her going quickly that way,
She wasn't enjoying her life.
I'll tell you after I find out today,
You could cut the air with a knife.

I loathe him for what he's doing to me.
They're so close to agreeing a price.
You ring him right now to find out the fee,
It's all on the roll of the dice.

You'd think they'd finally sort it by now,
The forms were the old ones, they said.
The funeral's on Friday, half-three, at Slough,
I'm tired and ready for bed.

She

Silent, sure and slowly now does Eden's shimmering sun,
Rise supreme, serenely, over summer season's bowers.
The skylarks, swifts and swallows skim the sky in serenades,
And silver shine the silken leaves of sanctifying trees.

The sheep, in peaceful fleeces, sleep still-standing in the shades,
So sweet the simple-scented flowers, languishing the hours.
Scarce any breeze to stir the Garden's sedges by the stream,
Or silence even soothing sounds of nectar-seeking bees.

Satin-smooth the shiny skins of orchard's bounteous apples,
So succulent and russet-rosy, strung from stretching boughs.
They seem to Adam's cynicism, speak of love's deceit,
And sharper than a serpent's fangs, still-born of jealousies.

But Eve, a sly and single sprite, then shows to him the prize,
Selected from the Sacred Tree that Knowledge disallows.
She offers such, that shown by God, she was to strictly shun,
Thus Adam's apple sticks in throats, Man's pleas are ill at ease.

So sour their taste I realize, so soon I score regrets.
Some siren sings her secret spells, such passions soon arouse.
Repents my soul, my spirit sick, my side she soon forsook,
She lays not in my sated arms in shallow phantasies.

Sad sorrows seems such just desserts, Eve's singular mistake,
She lost that sacred Paradise since using secret powers.
She toils and spins, her distaff state, in pain she bears her child,
Yet she I love, her smiles and charms, and she I shall but please!

The Old Cottage

Un-even flags, well-worn, that draw towards the door,
through tangled mass of fever-few and grass knee-high.
Almost hid by yew, crab-apple, dog-rose riot,
the tiny cottage sits, an old hay-barn nearby.

On bent, age-hardened baulks of oak from ships long gone,
the sullen, thick, grey slates by lichen forced to smile.
Crude, crumbling sandstone stack, its blue wood-smoke no more,
on mullioned windows blinks a shadowed-glass sundial.

Then enter in, and view the frugal hearth-place nook,
climb steep and narrow stairs that lead to chambers mean.
Be still, and listen to the echoes from the past,
of birth, death, joy, and pain, and lovers met, unseen.

The silent place still smiles its memories of old.
Forgotten people sitting warm by ashes cold.

Arbor Low

What mean these stones?
What marking-out achieves?
The rampart and the cast-out ditch in circularity.
The place deserted now, where once so many,
so much discussed, and traded more
A meeting place, so sacred, and secure?

The stretching plain of green and groves of ash.
The hunter and the hunted, life and death,
and bones that ran, or lay.
A human ring of time,
ellipsed and broken, joined,
parted, and then re-joined again
in links of blood and sweat and love.
The graves of great, in mounds.
The rest, unknown.

Viewed now in educated guess,
a scientific cold conjecture,
the simple ring still keeps its secret,
spinning on.
It moves beneath the sun,
as earth moves with it, tilting in its run.
A greater ring, in axis to the greater planes.
Turning in the heavens, day on day.

The pull of certainty remains,
the certainty of what?....
A will that bettered beasts,
and took control of destiny.
A will that brought these stones,
shaped and set them, and still remain,
and still retain that mass
of linking power throughout each age.

What mean these stones?
Cannot you guess?
Do you not yearn to leave your mark?
To join the ring and link?
Will your stones last so long?
O man, live on!

Landscape

I go there, sometimes.
The path leads me back down the years.
Treading slowly, in thoughts,
then quickly back again, to reality..

Memories; those mind pictures that haunt
and catch you out when least aware.
Summer flowers, Winter logs, .. rich, black hair,.. embers of love.
All flashing together with the sunlight stabbing through the leaves.
Laughter of another time, drifts of a half-forgotten snow.
Clouds of the past shadowing my search.

Changed. All changed.
The old gate has dragged a ridge in the pathway,
and is now locked, a padlocked chain, sullen and obstinate.
How often I swung on that gate, ..a young boy.
The stile is brambled over now; grass grows high.
How often we climbed that stile, the grass flattened on both sides then,
as the owls watched us, and the foxes barked.

I am changed.
My hair is grey-flecked, yet your smile is the same.
My legs are heavy on the path; but you run nimbly in front.
When you get to the gate, you open it easily and go through.
It swings shut with a clack that jolts my ears.
Then, all the times, in the thousands of times, that I heard it,
swell into a single thunderclap of shutting.

When I get to the gate, I stop, and stare down the path,
my face contorts as my hands touch the deadening chain.
You run on ahead, turn, and wave down the years.
Then, putting your hands to your brow to shield the glare of the sun,
you see that I have gone, and turn slowly away.
I watch you fade, and ache.
Never did I think we'd meet again,
and in such a way.

The path has disappeared, I cannot go there now.
Grass has covered it over, ivy has swallowed the gate.
We may remember,
but will not meet again.

Magpie Mine   *In the White Peak, Derbyshire*

Viewed from half a mile away,
the lanes surrounding,
keeping a respectful distance
from its monument of sullen grey.
An involved huddle of wasted walls,
half-roofs, gables, blind windows
and pylonic chimney stacks.
A gaunt, grim headstone to the grave of lead.
Unique, foreboding,
heavy in it's past.
Yet, also with a strange romanticness,
Even after all those painful years.

Once, a hum of industry,
a hive of unsweet wealth.
The slowly-poisoned sweat of men
that soaked the spoil-heaps,
and aged their backs too soon.
Fed their wives and children on bitter pittance,
begrudged by togas, cowls or wigs and silk
that knew not of it, or even cared.

Yet now, it stands, storm-blown and ravaged,
a heritage of when we used to slave,
a place of necessary bondage.
Today, a mere distraction,
an afternoon's short visit
for our history's experience,
hands-on, without the callouses.

Close your eyes
hear the thud of hammers,
watch the candle's glint,
back to sandaled feet and Latin tongues,

smell the hissing glow of molten ore,
haul dull-stamped pigs to wash away the sins of Empire
in plumbed and marble baths of cleansed sophistication,
and lay the drains that leech the dross of guilt.

see the smelt, cathedral-roofing rolls
to shield the wrath of God,

120

hung on carved and vaulting oak,
keeping dry the soaring pillars,
which echoed to Gregorian chant
from simple habits,
and over-zealous rain.
gaze on fettered glass of noble homes,
rich in hangings, art and gilded wood,
criss-crossing mullioned dawns
and dusks of perfect parks.

bind the crystal cups for wine,
reflect in Vauxhall mirrors,
and dance to blazing chandeliers.

hear the crack of muskets
and the cannon's grape-shot whine,
from Civil war or brave Trafalgar.
feel the boiling sea and blood-soaked cloth,
dredge up the bitterest notion man can make.
take up arms, aim your screaming death,
and live or die.

We're here because of them.

Now, look around,
and hear the deafening absence of this place.
This last memorial to the plateau's soul.
These silent walls imprisoning an empty tomb.
Yet, whispering ghosts and broken spirits tell us:
Keep away, you are not welcome here.
Ashamed, alone, these deep, dark, sucked-out
veins of Derbyshire.

Time to go;
Leave this sanctity of strive or starve,
its lonely thorns and shrouding mists,
its struggle; uneconomic, dangerous and dead.

Leave these haggard, windswept archives,
watched over by a single guard,
clad in black and white array.
An emblematic, sorrowing, single bird,
in the shadow of a barren womb.

My Rock

I used to climb up there, when once a boy,
and feel the sun, the rain, frost, wind, and dew.
To try and clear what I could not see through,
my mood within not always one of joy.

For then the questions that were on my mind
were more than all the answers in my book.
The ache of who I was, and where to look,
the blank of why, and what to leave behind.

While ill at ease on summit's grass I lay,
my inner arguments and dreams denied,
I gazed the valley's length from side to side,
and vowed that I'd return some future day.

And then I hope the light will shine the best,
On this small limestone hill, my Everest.

Trio

From noise and crowds and traffic fumes
I ever long to flee.
But theatres, pubs and book-lined rooms
are cities' hold on me!

Though solitude's my lonely state,
wild moor, green field, and tree.
The smell of hay and lark's elate,
this countryside is me!

Where wheeling gulls on stiff sea-breeze,
and boats, the tides decree.
When gale subsides in sunset ease,
the salty life's for me!

Buxton Market, 1913   *on reading Thomas Hardy's "The Breaking of Nations"*

They drive to market; down from the quiet, distant hills,
their panniers weather-bleached and filled with cooling bread,
the piebald, half-legged cob uncomplaining in its dull-hooved clops.
slow-spinning fellies, creaking elm and slapping leather straps.
Martha, up before the sun, has tied her hair in ribbons,
half-heartedly completed when seen and held to scorn.
These, her yellow secrets, bought with last week's haggled coins,
which false complaints about her wares her honest purse depleted.
Her dour husband, caring little and his temper never long,
always eager for the barrel-house, stops once along the way,
and finds his stick, ditch-left and lost the week before.
Young William, for the whole, full, fractious morning,
nurdling, with his hand held to his ear,
his wooden toy denied, a slap received.
The town is reached, already humming at its trade,
crowds all churning, milling, shouts of "*two-a-penny!*"
Stalls and canvas, loaded choice for nodding heads.
Bonnets, boots, black shawls and waistcoats bright with chains.
People chaffing, jostling in the hive of barter,
gostering at last week's bargains,
winked, and now half price;
a fool is he who never learns.
Impatient cattle, fly-frabbed, whisking, stand and wait
or stamp to the cobble's dusted heat,
sweat smelling, muzzle-dripped and tired.
A group of women gather round a wild-eyed zealot,
who calls "The End is Nigh!", his shaking fist held high.
Another trader simply mutters, "*Ar, b'non 'till th'sun's gone dairn!*"
and grins his neighbour's groaning, still-stacked board.
Yet, finally, her bread is sold, the counted coins twice-checked
and changed for this week's bag of flour, fine-sieved and snowed.
The disappointment still to come, when sadly split on reaching home.
Young William stares, then starts and winces for the dozing cob,
his father's stick hard struck, and better never found.
Martha, weary, looks up towards the gathering storm,
climbs the float's warped, wooden tailboard,
and notices her hands, so worn, and raw, and old.

cob – a light horse,   fellies – cart wheel rims,   barrel-house – the tavern
nurdling – whimpering, gostering – staring uncomprehendingly,
frabbed – annoyed, float - a small farm-cart
"Ar, b'non 'till th'sun's gone dairn!" -"Yes, but not until the sun has gone down!

Salford Quays

High up, a bird's eye view,
looking to the glow of a sunken sun.
A clear and rainbow-layered sky,
from flame to pale of indigo,
stretching over far Welsh hills.
Spread beneath, wider than the focus,
come trembling pinpricks of Salford's lights,
Broad flats of greying squares,
each with its numbered patterns of glow-worm dots,
like luminous dominoes, chequered, played out
on some vast, crowded gaming-board of life and chance.
Chameleon to the whim of commerce,
the famine and the glut of trade,
its years both kind and cruel.
And there, below, clear-running to the centre,
the very soul, a slick aorta to it's feeding heart,
The Great Canal, cooling from the west horizon,
sparkling in the eastern moon,
another moon bathing within.
A city calming itself for rest,
the brushstrokes finished, the canvas dry.

Gone, the cobbles,
soaked with sweat and sooted rain,
the blackened, red-brick rows.
Gone, the shawls and mothers,
working on the looms and shuttles,
who pawned and scrubbed their lives away.
Gone, the caps and men,
that forged and hammered,
fought and gambled, then went back for more.
Apprenticed, bonded, factory-whistled in and out,
clogged-up, clocked-in, locked-out, and doled,
their brief release in ale and sex.
And gone the courting couple,
hand in hand, along the cut,
love aching, life wearied.
Their self-replacing children proudly born,
in spite of rickets, coal and riveting machines.
Willing Saturday's freedom hooter,
gazing on Sunday's bleeding heart.
Till, shrouded in the very cotton,
washed clean by tears,
finally buried, with ham.

- Comedy and Parody -

The Holiday

Passport-passed, jab-protected, we crowd on the planes,
flying off on vacation, from stresses and strains.
We needed a break, and so booked on the 'net',
the hotel seems friendly, though not finished yet.

Adequate food, drinks inclusively-paid,
"Though-not-quite-as-nice-as-the-last-place-we-stayed."
Round the pool, sun-tanned bodies, all lying in rows,
some supine, others prone, like sardines, head-to-toes.

Levelled out, oiled and boiled, in the heat of the sun,
every skin-type, from pale, to the well-over-done.
Stretched taut, or relaxed, with a few that are sagging,
asleep, or excited, loose tongues all a-wagging.

Customised hairstyles, bright-coloured and braided,
factor ten sun-cream, eye's fashionably shaded.
Indulgent and languid, detached, yet aware
of their neighbour's sly glance, trying hard not to stare.

Full-stomached, or dieting, gym-work-out honed,
'six-pack', or puny, and all mobile-phoned.
With their personal stereos plugged in their ears,
they'll all be stone deaf, long before they're old dears.

Round the edge strut young men, oh-so-casual and firm,
new tattoos, henna-drawn, for the holiday term.
All those beautiful girls in bikini swim-wear,
though the cost, per square inch, by proportion, unfair.

While some just decide that they really don't care,
put their thighs in a thong, and go toplessly bare.
Older men, then pretend that they're reading their books,
wish their waistlines were less, but their wives are good cooks.

While drink-sodden louts, full of duty-free haul,
'bomb' in the pool, causing havoc for all.
Ladies, who'd rather their partners were single,
just wiggle their hips, as relationships mingle.

Moon-lit-walks, on-the-beach, full-of-sangria-bold,
vacation romances so soon to grow cold.
Oh, every-one's desperate for someone to love,
or have passionate sex, from below, or above.

The fort-night's soon over, so pack up your bags,
delay at the airport that endlessly drags
We've spent all our euros, and tipped all the staff,
with a big straw sombrero, still game for a laugh.

Down to earth, with a bump, to the rain, how we sighed,
while away, back at home, the poor goldfish had died.
All spent up, now we wait for the holiday snaps.
Shall we go back next year? Not quite sure, well, perhaps!

Sale-Fever

I must go down to the sales again, B.& Q. and M.F.I.
And all I ask is a Top Shop, and a Selfridges nearby,
And the Kookai, and the Woolworths, to Boots and Specs Savers,
And a Monsoon on the C.& A. , Next to Quicksavers

I must go down to the sales again, to the Harvey Nicholls queue,
The M.& S., and the D.F.S., and maybe Debenhams too,
And all IKEA, All Sports, and Bay, with a Super-Drug flying,
And a New Look, at the Body Shop, Argos-catalogue-buying.

I must go down to the sales again, to the F.C.U.K. life,
To John Lewis, and to Harrods, with all the world and his wife;
And all I want is a plastic card, and a sell-by-date decoder,
And two new feet, and a facial scrub, at the free make-over

The Menu

Balsamic, wild mushrooms and goat's cheese,
with a salad of rocket and thyme.
Some virginal oil of olive, please,
on courgettes, with a garnish of lime.
A seasonal forest-fruits coulis,
some pan-fried monkfish tails.
Vegetarian, or vegan, crème brulee,
liver pate of organic quails.

What happened to dumplings and suet?
Where custard and hot spotted dick?
When the gravy was starred, as I knew it,
and the jam was home-made and thick.
What happened to brawn and fat bacon?
Home-cured ham on hooks in the hall?
Why has cream on the milk been taken?
And strawberries have no taste at all?

Fajitas, paninnis and pasta,
Stir-fried, or nouvelle cuisine.
Kebabs, Thai, Balti and Rasta
Or Mexican Chilli terrine.
Bagels and Sushi and Bhuna,
Sun-dried tomatoes and soy.
Where is the food I'd far sooner
eat, yesterday, when I was a boy?

Oh, for some rhubarb crumble,
thin currant bread, mushy peas!
Oh, for the plain and the humble
scone, hot from the oven, please!
Home-grown beef and Yorkshire pud,
With English mustard smeared.
Thick porridge, tripe-and-onions would
make you a man to be feared.

But its takeaway Chinese and fondue,
humus, gezpacho and dill.
Barbecued squid and French ragout
on the Two Star Michelin bill.
I've eaten the smallest of portion,
three plates were under each course,
and so to the wind I'll throw caution,
I could bloody well eat a horse!

If you find a feather

If you find a feather, pick it up.
You've nothing to lose,
just put it in your pocket,
one you don't much use,
or better still,
a pocket that you never ever choose.

You might not see it then for quite a while,
but when you do, you'll declare
you don't remember
the time you put it there,
or who you were with,
or where.

If you find a feather, pick it up,
I always do.
I put it in my pocket,
to remind me of you.
I know it's rather silly, but I do.
It's not superstition, it's not weird,
It's not something to be feared,
it just shows an oddity,
in my character, or two.

The dry-cleaners must have laughed
when they found a feather in my pocket.
They must think I'm daft.
Unless….. they did the same
that very morning,
in which case I'll claim
they're just the same as me,
just as daft, you see.

A feather in my pocket.

Some people call them angels.

Recruits

Down the openness of no-man's land,
faces set, fixed, to the beat of aggression.
Out from behind the defence, the shielding,
with pampered innocence of basic training,
an insufficient grounding, left behind.
Young, so very young, yet arrogant, dismissive,
ready for the first,
or the finale.

And they, waiting, on either side,
with traps of ambush, critical, fatally condescending.
The studied expressions of surprise and attack,
perhaps begrudgingly impressed by the advance,
yet focused on the baiting, with time enough to choose.
Mock praise for the limitless lines,
but not for the stupidity.

Yet still coming more, wave after wave,
more new recruits, contemptuous in cold bravado,
new uniforms, untried.
Immature physiques, honed undersize,
lacking the scars of experience,
or battle-hardened wisdom.
So many, taking up their positions
of vulnerability, staring impassively,
their boots in step, comrades coerced together.

And they wait for them, ammunition to pay,
eyes that narrow in the glare of flood-lights,
waiting for the ultimate in confrontation.
Their decision to choose,
who, what and when.
Fixing on their target,
fingers tense in expectation,
and then, a deafening roar,
a thousand hands claw out
in jealous need to claim,
raw envy ever-growing
for the spoils.

Dressed to kill, a battle to die for.
War paint and rags. The fashion show.

Coronation

I were asked "What's yer first recollection?"
Well fer me that's an easy decision,
I were watchin' th'Queen's Coronation,
int' front room, on our first television.

Me Father 'ad gone out an' bought one,
proper posh, in me'og'ny veneer.
He couldn't quite really afford it,
so 'e gave up his fags an' 'is beer.

He just 'ad enough fer t'deposit,
th' rest were ont' th'twelve-monthly plan.
From Curry's it were, in Spring Gardens,
two young men brought it out in a van.

"We're Technicians," they said "come to fix up your set"
and took off the wrappings, all action,
till it stood there in all of it's glory,
but Mother said, "What a contraption!"

Now the name of the set was an 'Alba',
wi' two doors, behind which, were a screen
that were six inches 'igh, 'an six inches wide,
made 'o glass, curved funny, an' pea-green.

Mother said "It dun't go wi' me curtins,
an' me'og'ny, well, that's a joke,
It's too red, far too big, an' too 'modern',
an' besides, all me furniture's oak."

On the set, at the front, were four little knobs
made o' 'Bacolite', black, shiny, and round,
"On", "Vertical Hold", "Horizontal", as well,
and, "Volume" to turn up the sound.

"Well I think it's ugly" said Mum, in a huff,
an' folded 'er arms, wi' a frown.
"You'll not say that in a bit," returned Dad,
"Watchin' Queen, th'Archbishop an' th'Crown."

Well they couldn't agree where to put it at first,
then decided int' corner o'th room,
Then mother got vexed an' said "How'd yer expec'
me t' sweep behind that wi' me broom."

Then younger technician went out fer a while,
so perplexed, Father said, "Where's 'e gone?"
"Up ont' chimney" said th'older one, beamin' a smile,
"Fixin' aerial, so th'picture comes on."

Well they finally got it all set up to go,
an' we sat crowded round ont' th'settee.
But th'screen stayed like snow, and Mother said "Oh,
"Well, I'll best go get buns an' brew tea."

Me Father were livid, an' started to shout,
both Technicians looked red and embarrassed.
They fiddled wi' knobs, then gi' it a clout,
yer could tell they were getting quite 'arassed.

Father took a step back, then he let out a yell,
his patience by this time were thin.
Then he picked up the thing that he'd trodden upon,
an' said "I think yer might first plug it in"

The set were connected; we all held our breath,
it flickered and blinked for a while.
Then all of a sudden it come on at last,
an' th'Technicians give Father a smile.

Mother came back with the tea on a tray,
to the sight of the pageant so grand,
There were Coach, an' 'orses, flags wavin' away,
an' th'Life Guard's an' Milit'ry Band.

In Westminster Abbey descended an 'ush,
when th'Archbishop poured th'oil ont' Queen's 'ead.
"Vivat Regina!" said Lords, in their plush,
"I'll bet that Crown's heavy," Dad said.

Th'procession went back in great splendour and state
To th'Palace, for th'balcony scene.
I'll never forget it fer rest o' my life,
It felt just as though as I'd been.

When I'm asked what my first recollection would be,
In my mind is a wonderful scene.
Of nineteen hundred and fifty-three,
June the second an' "God Save The Queen!"

Slagging-off the New Restaurant

The "New Excess", the smell of success,
from thinking and planning and doing.
All the best–laid schemes, the hopes and the dreams,
by the upwardly-mobile-reviewing

A new restaurant, for the garde-avant,
the hoi-polloi, and the glitz!
A gap in the niche for the nouveau-riche
who wouldn't be seen at The Ritz.

The smart décor, the laminate floor,
the mock leather seats and the murals.
Such elegant soirees, with invited gourmets
and the drapes in designer-led florals.

White marbled floors, and smoky-glass-doors,
with the whizz and the fizz of 'Champoo'.
The under-floor-lighting, in mirror-delighting
and gold-plated taps in the loo.

The well-turned-of-heel, read in fashionable spiel,
in today's glossy-must-have-new-mags.
All those delicate ravers, some new-curried favours
with the latest posh-labelled handbags.

The great-party-bashers, and boorish-gate-crashers,
all taxied, both to, and away.
Quite the best thing in town, with no hint of a frown,
where the steaks are divinely flambé.

And the chic cabaret will subtly play,
as the critics are watered and fed.
From the presses have rolled their reviews of pure gold,
that, hopefully, give some street cred.

Now the party is over, the guests, so un-sober,
have crawled off to home in the gloom.
The chef has erupted, the owners bankrupted,
and the dish has run off with the spoon.

And the next eating-place will open apace,
with exactly the same hue-and-cry.
Gastronomic deceivers, like financial receivers,
pick your bones, and your wallets, quite dry.

The Tale Of The Two Three-Toed Sloths

A sad and lonely three-toed sloth
Lived all alone in undergrowth
He longed to wed and plight his troth
Forever pledge his marriage oath
To some young, single, female sloth
Then he met her in a bush
Smiling sweetly with a blush
In his heart he felt a flush
But his luck he dare not push
Being a sloth he could not rush
He knew not how to show
How much he loved her so
His heart in fiery glow
And desperate to know
Her answer, yes or no.
So he bought a ring
On his knee must bring
She to him did cling
Tears of joy to wring
Fixed a date in spring
White dress display
Suit, morning grey
In church to pray
I do, must say
A perfect day
Wedding oath
Headdress blowth
Champagne flowth
Bouquet throwth
Rapture knowth
Coyness
Undress
Mattress
Caress
Impress
Slowth
Slowth
Quick
Quick
Slowth

133

Curtains

If, at your window you have no curtain,
And decision is hard, or just uncertain,
Then pause awhile, and ponder this,
Professional advice would not go amiss.

Do you favour dramatic, simple or plain?
Does your window look out at a view, or a pain?
What sort of effect do you want to impart?
Elegante, or twee, or state-of-the-art?

You can block out the light with different kinds
Of roller, Venetian, or Roman blinds,
They're all very well, if your budget is keen,
But not quite right for the drawing-room scene.

Voile is so "in", though damask is old hat,
And no-one says curtains, it's "drapes", and that's that.
Chintz is so dated, and velvet is out,
And William Morris with G-plan will shout.

How about satin?, or silk?, or chenille?
It all depends on the mood that you feel.
Brocade is quite classy, and suede can be chic,
Laura Ashley is stunning, but well past its peak.

The language of "drapes" is a world of its own,
Inspired by "design", and a bit over-blown.
Tie-backs, and hems, and tassels refining.
Fullness, and drop, and fleece inter-lining,

Homely or grand, the result is amazing,
Material so thick, you'll not need double-glazing.
Rouching and rufflette, poles and rails,
Headings and pelmets, and swags-and-tails.

One-and-a-half-times-the-width-if-it's-net,
But-two-and-a-half-for-the-drapes-don't-forget.
The creases will fall, when they've hung for a while,
The lead weights will help, a good choice for the style.

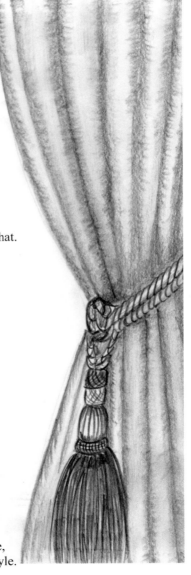

134

Poplin or muslin? Velour or sateen?,
Rayon or dralon? Or rich velveteen?.
Brushed cotton or corduroy? Full-length or short?
Made-to-measure? Or off-the-peg bought?

They're treated you see, so they really can't shrink,
What's that mark? Oh my God, it's biro, I think!
When they're drawn, how cosy to shut out the night,
Or fling back next morning, and welcome the light.

They'll cost you a fortune, an arm and a leg,
To keep up with 'The Jones's', steal, borrow or beg.
But drapes are important, choose fabric with care,
Then pay your Designers to make you a pair.

Pearls

Shine, shine, lunescent regularity,
your abacus of rosary delight,
in counting up each luscious time of sin
when worn by her who courts prosperity.
Once mermaid's tears, that sank below the swells
and caught in oyster beds among the rocks.
Those salted drops from siren's eyes lament,
which never dried, once captured in their shells.

Gleam, gleam, in nacre'd singularity,
your circling chain of modesty reviled.
Deep-dived and hungered-for rich prize below,
from sacrificial mothers, born to live.
Soft-manacled by silk, by others coarsely warmed,
for her that languishes in gaudy show.

Cheap token of her immorality.

Children

Their loud, brash music, raucous unwashed look,
the curfews broken, and so seldom brought to book.
"I'm starving!" or "I've really got to go!",
no hat or coat in Winter's frost and snow.

"Can you lend, till Thursday, just five quid?
I need to put on Ebay just one more bid."
"Just drop me here, I promise not to be too late,
but don't wait up, 'cos this is our second date."

"There's eight of us, the kitchen we all share,
The cleaning's done in rota, so it's fair."
"Jill, Beth, me, and Amy, who really is a dear,
John, Will, Zak and Harry, who thinks he might be queer."

Gone, school uniform of grey and braid and white,
now 'designer-led', fake-holed and garish-bright.
Short back and sides and pigtails banned from view,
now streaked and gelled, blonde, dipped in red or blue.

Your car is always empty on the petrol gauge,
they tell you that it's so 'un-cool' to be a sage.
The simple bag of sweets are swapped for smokes,
the skipping rhymes for condoms and blue jokes.

They say you're old, you know you're middle-aged
but you can always pay, for they are so 'un-waged.'
And yet I envy them their vigour and their youth,
my fat, and thinning hair, I hate, and that's the truth.

Out to Lunch

on the Brecon Beacons

The talk is easy and the weather fine,
how good to lunch and taste the wine!
Four friends in harmony incline,
beneath The Walnut Tree's sweet sign!

A Short Discourse on Welsh Noses

The diversity of the Welsh nose has often been the source of lively discussion for many years. Geographically speaking they fall into two groups, the 'local' and the 'even more local'. Medically, these unusual breathing and smelling protuberances are viewed with great interest. Measurements taken of adult noses over many years have shown neither shrinkage nor growth. However, "true to type" seems to be a common denominator in the known varieties and areas where they are to be found.

There is a certain type of nose which often appears westwards of a line between Caernavon and Pwllheli. This is a genetic mutation of unusual length, thinness and also curiously pointed. Best viewed from sideways on, in profile, this nose is known as The "Lleyn Peninsula."

A very different nose sometimes occurs, though it does sometimes skip a generation, in the coastal areas between St. Davids and Milford Haven. Best observed from the front, this nose is strongly inclined to the left. Taken in context of points of the compass, it is easy to see why this particular nose is tabulated as the rare and noble "Haverfordwest."

Two classic noses, the origin of which follows, were first seen after a celebrated 18th Century Bare Knuckle Fight. This was between that famous protagonist "Pem Shire", - a burly 'Southpaw' fisherman using his famous 'Fishguard' defence stance, and the notorious "Wem Breacon", - a huge, dark-haired sheep farmer, also known as 'The Black Mountain of South Wales.' The upshot of the fight was declared a draw after Pem broke one of Wem's teeth just as Wem gave Pem a nasty nosebleed. This gave rise to The "Pembroke-shire" and The "Breacon Beacon" noses respectively.

There is a very pretty type of nose often seen nowadays in females to the east of the Snowdonia region. Much favoured by comprehensively educated young ladies of the same Christian name, this is the pert, little "Bety's-wy-Coed."

Some people on the North Welsh Coast have a propensity to catarrh. This can be an unpleasant affliction, especially when one is preparing leeks for supper. The strong, oniony aroma can cause some noses to run uncontrollably, and usually when one hasn't got a handkerchief. These resourceful people often use their sleeves. However, it has been recorded that prolonged use of the wrist and lower arm in such circumstances can sometimes result in the nose acquiring a turned-up 'C'-shape, or 'retrousse' appearance. Medically, this nose is referred to as "The Colwyn Bay" but is caused by repetitive syndrome, rather than dominant genes.

Though certainly there is a well-documented paper recording one particularly fertile family moving from this area to the West Welsh coast. They took this unfortunate blocked nasal problem with them, giving rise to the increasingly common nose seen now called the "Abe-ryst-wyth-on-Cardigan." - Abe, use your sleeve boyo!

By far the most musical nose is the one that is blown with such discrete cultured sounds at the world-famous Eisteddfod. Surely only the dulcet tones of the wonderful Welsh Harp or melodious Welsh Choir can surpass the subtle sonority emanating from the nostrils of a well-blown "Llangollen."

The only other nose of note is the rather coarser sounding "Bangor."

I commend this short treatise to Your Lordships.

Rap Parody on 'Kubla Khan' by S. T. Coleridge

Dealer

In tax-free isle did the 'Main Man'
a multi-million mansion plan.
From Class-A drugs Colombian.
Through laundered money
He would be in luxury
down by the tropical sea.

His distribution, like no other,
of E-pills, smuggled under cover,
would buy Him power, provide His lover.
His silk-suit and His Lear jet, would be
designer idiosyncrasy.

A playboy's dream, stretch-limocars,
With bowling lanes, jacuzzi spas,
Where manicured, tanned beauties curled,
and 'snow' was sniffed through dollars furled,
by fountain of ecstasy.

Armed heavy-mob, with facial scars
and pony tails, ex-prison bars,
a cold menagerie.
To guard his secret, evil world,
the paparazzi's cameras hurled
into His private sea.

But you pay the price of leisure,
more and more the habit craves.
Razor-cut a bigger measure,
then 'main-lining' soon enslaves.
Hallucinating waves of pleasure
floating down to icy graves.

A young girl with a future bright
in a nightmare, there, I saw her.
Looking for adventurous night.
dancing in the 'Club Abora',
There the music loud and long
a tidal wave of deafening song
Rocked in caves of burning ice
His 'Wonder-drome' of hidden vice.

And all who took no notice there,
that should have said, "Take care, beware,
His flashy clothes, His stylish hair
For if He offers, then think twice,
tomorrow's dawn may see you dead."
For He on innocence has fed
and drunk the blood of Merchandise.

Metric Tonnes

I try to write a weighty sonnet, where
Iambic stressed pentameters unstress.
Containing subject matter; Love, so fair.
Hyperbole trochaic not digress.

Enjambment, also, must be given space
To link these lines, and give the metre wit.
Attribute anapaest and dactyl grace,
With octave and a sestet, volte split.

I thought there was such ease in writing verse,
Yet now I sit dumbfounded, and in shock,
These fourteen lines now haunt me like a curse,
My pen thrown down from guilt and writer's block.

All Shakespeare and Petrachan sonnets rhyme,
Ten feet of metric stanza quite sublime.

The Emperor's Reception on Global Warming

Dear Prime Minister,
                     I haven't seen you in *ages*.
I simply *had* to tell you of this year's Reception.
        Well, of course, one had to be *officially* invited, and I *was*,
they don't just ask *anyone*, as you know,
On your behalf I tendered your apologies, *as instructed*.
        This year's themed decor was, again, *white*.
I mean, why would anyone *think* of changing?
        The catering was, *de rigueur*, smorgasbord,
so much more civilised than all that clumsy silver service,
though again, as *last* year, the menu had a propensity towards fish.
Surprisingly the portions were *tiny*, dare one say *economics* has raised its ugly head?
        I rather thought they had invited *too* many though,
the crush was *rather* off-putting,
and some *did* start to jostle for *position*.
Manners are *everything*, don't you think?
        However the weather was kind, almost *tepid*,
as many said, most *unseasonably* so.
        There *were* one or two grumblings about the *venue* - smaller than usual.
Alarmingly, the *less-enlightened* suggested *dropping* the stuffy dress code?!
I *ask* you, standards *must* be preserved at *all* costs,
Once you allow *lounge* suits, it's all over.
Black tie or *nothing*. Next thing it will be *shell suits*!
Tradition must *not* be compromised.
        I found *so* many old friends from the past there,
it was *delightful*, though sadly, very few *young* people.
Comforting to see the trendier sorts *not* represented.
Unfortunately, one or two undesirables *were* lurking on the periphery,
I afraid 'non u' is beginning to be a *slight* worry.
        However, nothing could really spoil the evening,
Seeing one's *friends*, chatting pleasantly,
avoiding controversial *issues*.
After all, we are there to *enjoy* ourselves.
        The only *slight* concern was, *regrettably*,
a *noticeable* lack of snow.
Definitely the icebergs were *much* smaller,
and *towards the end* we did all feel somewhat *jaded*.
        One old friend joked that he hadn't seen a polar bear for *months*.
But the odd thing was, no-one laughed. What *is* the world coming to?
        Hope to see you *next* year, *Deo volente*.
                                  Yours respectfully,
                                       A. Penguin.

What am I?

For Kings, in gilded silver borne,
in time, watched, running free.
In taste, to savour all. Forlorn,
the tears of many a sea.

In laughter's furthest length it lies,
and custom's thieving pound.
In wages of some earlier ties,
dredged up from depths profound.

A fool, in statue frozen still,
ill-turned and backward leaned
For sins of twins in evil, will
remain, and un-redeemed.

The seller's cure, whose eye is blind,
is an Arab potentate.
To keen the blander, fattened kind,
yet heart will violate.

Preserver, curing winter's track.
A tale of feathered mirth.
At clause benign, then rubs the back.
Takes not a peck of worth.

In kilted pottage recipe,
more sacred than the scone.
In careless spills, best remedy
o'er shoulder sorrows thrown.

Above, below, in chance is born
man's station, rich or mean.
To know the truth, lest it not dawn.
St. Matthew, five, thirteen.

(Solution P.T.O.)

Solution: Salt.

An aristocrat's centrepiece, the gilding prevents the salt attacking the silver.
Used in an egg timer.
Flavours the feast
Salty tears

'I could have laughed till I cried.'
Salt tax.
The Centurion was paid partly in salt - 'salary' (Salarium = Roman = salt.)
Salt mine

Lot's wife turned into a pillar of salt
warned by God not to look back
at Sodom and Gomorrah
therefore, was not saved.

When the hole in the salt cellar is blocked
give it a shake (sheik).
Improves the 'fattened calf' – kine.
Heart attack.

To 'Salt-down' meat. For melting ice.
Putting salt on a bird's tail.
After the 'cat-o'-nine tails' punishment, rub salt into the wound.
Not worth a pinch of salt.

Porridge,
more vital than 'The Stone of Scone'
Spill salt, spill sorrow,
Throw some over your shoulder.

Denoted your birth status, or lineage,
e.g., at medieval banquets.
By now you've either got it …or had enough.
Biblical quote.

- Birds of a feather -

Morning at Llandegeman Fach

The sky held them up
in awe, no less than ours.
Two buzzards, circling in ease,
just under the clouds.

Majestic, serene and ageless,
indifferent to our jealous eyes,
yet not to those who chose
to ignore their feudal dues.

Sounding to one another
In eerie, mewing calls,
Recounting distant memories
of ancient steel and bloodied banners.
Passed down through parent's eyes
that once viewed man's small pageant.

In sculpted bronze they flew,
mapping the far horizons.
Coursed on vast and rounded pinions,
Inexorably scoring the valley's depths,
buoyed up and perfectly balanced
on the fathoms of August air.

The distant pillars of Skirrid
and Sugarloaf supporting
their noble, echoing court.
And we, mere tenants of their
Fiefdom's boast, looked up
and palled on their dynasty.

And did they even notice us
in the glory of their morning?

143

Kingfisher at Swainsley

Oh! How he mocks me with his flashing blue!
Snake-skims the stream in orange-bellied fires,
to lift the glutted trout his skill conspires.
This midget peacock, India's burning hue.
Assassin, silent-silked, reflects the gleam
of lazy pools and sun-lit riffled shales.
His bright, refracted dagger seldom fails,
no pity for the grayling's summer dream.
Aurora borealis midday-scanned,
he waits his chance of sure and sudden blow
to pin the scales of victim far too slow.
His vigil hid in chestnut's ponderous stand.
My box of flies, split cane and floating line,
riparian folly. Oh, your wings were mine!

Mallard

With hopeful, beady, hungry eye he swims a slow approach,
a collar, white, that sternest priest in truth could not reproach.
His iridescent emerald head with purple overlaid,
and yellow bill, a well-worn tool, his trusty dibbling spade.

His chestnut-pink enamelled front juts out in swelling prow,
he rises, flaps, then sails close-furled, as stately as a dhow,
The hull, so often water-proofed, glides easy on the lake.
and turns to port, the hidden oars leave ripples in his wake.

His grey great-coat, an Admiral's, the epaulettes discern.
a pigtail curl, defiant snooked, is proudly worn astern.
He comes ashore and waddles near in rolling Sea-dog gait,
and yet, I think a Buccaneer befits his pirate state,

I throw the crusts, and suddenly, an entire fleet descends,
these avian clowns, in rubber boots, on greed their luck depends.
The naval squadrons of the park, full mutiny declare,
be quick! Sir Drake, *quack-quack*, alack, in love and war all's fair!

144

Swan

An icing of lace
spun on cool, floating marble,
you know your own grace
and flaunt the ensemble.

In glowing candescence of avian lux,
parting the commerce of insolent ducks,
nodding coots and other inferior matter.
A regal, though singular, snobbish regatta.

In stiff affectation,
aesthetic, pure Parian,
with full-rigged perfection
of blue-blooded galleon.

Chiffon Cleopatra on ivory decks,
reflected on water with Siamese necks.
In mirroring crystal, with rippling wake,
a poised ballerina, the queen of the lake.

A dignified arching
of snaking throat drawn,
effete tutu starching,
superior scorn.

Yet angelic wings are all a disguise,
His power is rape, deceit and surmise,
The motive is carnal, beastly in lust,
the innocent tail a purposeful thrust.

For a god in false blushes
is this bird, for the mating,
and hidden by rushes
his Leda lies waiting.

The Owl

The Owl
is a fowl
with a haunting howl,
and a wise, bespectacled, feathery cowl.

He lives,
bespoke, in an English oak,
with several other woodland folk,
and a hole in the trunk for his head to poke.

This bird
has preferred
to be night-time heard,
and "Too-wit-to-whoo" is his favourite word.

His call
is not all
you'd expect to enthral,
and small nervous rodents on hearing it, pall.

His beak
gives a tweak
and the field-mice go "*squeak*!"
or hide in the grass, shivering silently, meek.

His eyes
are a size
that you cannot despise
while reflecting the moon in nocturnal surprise.

His claws
never pause
in his murderous cause,
and the miller then offers some grateful applause.

His wings
are the things
that death often brings
swooping silent in ambush, as midnight bell rings.

By day
in dismay
he roosts hidden away,
after dusk he returns for his ghostly foray.

At night
in his flight
he can give you a fright
as he flashes in front of your bicycle-light.

The Owl
is a fowl
of inscrutable scowl
and-unusual-ornithological-vowel!

Wild Geese

The faintest yet unmistakable sound
strains my ears in surprise,
concentrating,
then, relief in affirmation.
A sound, dripped in rare portions,
twice a year, either side of
Winter.

Coming from the north
with the falling leaf,
convincing,
in resolute urgency of
companionable wings, calling to each other.
A vee of slow, grey-feathered
lightning.

Warning clarions of bleak days,
snow and sullen gales,
imprisoning,
away to the waiting estuary.
A ritual of dependence,
and a promised
return.

Kestrel

Quivering silently, hanging on high,
patiently menacing, scorching the sky.
Lifting the wind on pinions proud,
trembling scimitar, cutting the cloud.
Feathering, fluttering, black on blue,
solitary, harrowing, riding the view.
Gravity scorning in lightning flash stoops,
seeking the vermin by harvested stooks.
Teasing the breeze in challenging height,
soaring in sunset, eclipsing the light.
Strafing the hedges, screening the hill,
watching the sedges, hovering still.
Stalking, suspended, floating on breath,
wickedly sharpened, certain in death.
Eager and tensioned, hunting by right,
Kestrel, the heavens belong to your flight!

Heron

Blue grey stillness
standing by the reeds,
slate carved statue
patient for his needs.
Thin legs stilting
sedges, hidden by
graceful willow,
humming dragonfly.
Slim poised hunter
silent by the pool,
brown trout quiver,
deep and dark and cool.
Snake coiled neckline,
cruel yellow eye,
Sharp long dagger
waiting by and by.
Prey comes swimming
ominously nigh,
long wait over,
lightning stab and die.

148

The Coot

Of all the watery birds to boot,
I think I rather like the coot.
There's something really quite absurd
about this black, pretentious bird.
It dons a cape theatrical,
and opera mask of white decal.
With scant regard for camouflage,
like sore thumb in a bad collage,
Its large, green, half-inflated boots
are what give me a fit of hoots,
For paddling underneath they're grand,
yet so ungainly on the land.
But I suppose they're what it needs
while gallivanting round the reeds.
And far from being a silent mute,
its call is like an off-key flute.
The other birds it seems to shun,
devoid of any sense of fun,
Prefers to live out on the edge
and pokes its bill in marshy dredge.
Its territory is defined,
and will defend if much maligned.
Intruders near its nest are chased,
thieving corvids splashed, outfaced.
It seems to live a single life,
not often seen as man and wife.
She, so peevish, prone to bicker,
he, a sanctimonious vicar.
And yet the river would be dull
without the coot's drab leg to pull.
A feathered clown in masquerade,
lampooned by rhyming pasquinade
Of all the watery birds to boot,
well, yes, I rather like the coot.

Birdcages

These yellow-painted gaudy prisons
reflected in the plate-glass prisms
of April sunshine. Pagodas, round, square, cushion-top,
hanging from the cast arcading of the high street shop.
Each with its plastic cup and plate,
with a pull-out tray to defecate.
Respective water, millet seed, and no regret
of the inmates need to fend for itself, to live and let.

What wrongful crime has been committed
the prisoner cannot be acquitted?
Wings unstretched and muted throat reviled,
plumage dulled and moulted head defiled.

Skies allow migrating panoply,
forests simply lend their canopy.
Bushes grant them squatters rights,
plains ignore their nesting sites.
Marshes yield and share their rush,
the dawning day demands no hush.

Who would buy these thin, vile bars
put out the nightingale's bright stars.
Pull the linnet from the bramble,
the shivering, moonlit night-owl strangle,
Why tear the blackbird from the bark,
or dry the wet, cascading lark.

These yellow cages, filled with drooping wings
and innocence, which never sings.

Reading

When my fingers unlock the keys of sound,
and my feet push down to subtly quieten,
or else to make thicker, blend and blur.
When my arms fall heavy, or gently alight,
my hands float in and out, or rise and fall,
the fine extremities caress or bend to will.
When my eyes go just in front of time,
and my ears follow the sounds, now heard,
of the mind of him who wrote the lines.
   Then, my conversation with Mozart, or Chopin,
   or any other sad, mad composer, begins.

When my fingers turn the fertile pages,
and my feet hang heavy from the hammock,
anchoring me in the quiet of the garden.
When my hands hold still the binding of the book,
my mind flying off to distant lands and times,
the sharp experience of love, or hate, or other.
When my eyes unravel and weigh the words
ad my ears listen to their reason following,
when all my senses tune to some awareness.
   Then, my conversation with Shakespeare or Lawrence,
   or any other sad, mad creator, begins.

When my fingers close around your own,
and my feet walk side by side with yours,
or stand toe to toe in earnest, face to face.
When our arms link, or hold, or catch,
and our hands touch gently, or take, or give,
those tender movements only known to us.
When our eyes close, no sight needed,
ears deaf, undismayed by want of sound,
the knowing mind and beating heart. Then,
   then, the words and music between you and I,
   like any other sad, mad lovers, begins.

Love

Our love is clear and sweetly heard,
like the simple thrill of a new-dawn bird.

Our love is warm and gently fanned,
like an ocean wave on Sri Lankan sand.

Our love is magic, dreaming or awake,
like the trembling moon in a shimmering lake.

Our love is gentle, moist, then still,
like an April shower on a Derbyshire hill.

Our love is soft and finely-spun,
like a christening-gown in the summer sun.

Our love is rich and nobly fine,
like honeyed grapes of Auslese wine.

Our love is intense and passion-sprung,
like ecstasy in La Boheme's aria sung

Our love is exquisite, serene, profound,
like rapturous joy of Rachmaninov's sound.

Our love is forever, shown and told,
like the promised vow in ring of gold,

Our love is total, complete and sure.
that, unlike death, lives evermore

The fourth Harry Potter film and what I would not like changed

A decision taken lightly, diversion required.
The journey well known and, up to this, uneventful.

The purring engine, effortlessly over the moor,
not intruding on a well-loved C.D., lyrics joined in.

The fourth "Harry Potter" film expectantly discussed
with youthful glee, yet senior control.

And then you said, out of the blue,
"What, about me, would you not like changed?"

I laughed, and teased "Good dinners!"
Then I sensed your mood, the question repeated.

"Not your physicality, not your smile, nor the caring and sharing."
Then it dropped from my lips in electric simplicity;

"Your integrity…, in all things."
"Thank you," you said, and smiled.

I wondered how I could have struggled for all of five seconds,
"Yes, your integrity," I repeated slowly, and smiled back.

A question asked, chaffed, repeated and answered.
And an even deeper bond was tied.

The film was not up to expectation,
but our world was better for that conversation.

To his love

Your eyes look into mine, into my heart,
where only you can sit, where room for one.
Our times, now running past so swift, are gone
before we have enough to count, and part.

Your hand, when baking bread or setting flowers,
or holding book, or linen wash and furl,
so strong, yet still a lady, still a girl,
so gentled, whether dull or playing hours.

Your voice, in sense of honour, art, or songs,
rolls back the days too heavy in their worth,
and calms, supports, in sadness, or in mirth,
gives me the certainty to each belongs.

Encouragement, the watchword of our love;
the blood of lion, the softness of the dove.

Mild rebuked

Let this blank page speak out of whom I love,
my Lady, who delights me with her charms.
'Tis she, steadfast, lies ever in my arms,
her company, rejoiced, ne'er tiring of.

She speaks and does her life's integrity
with words and deeds. Full fair to all she shows.
Yet mild rebukes, full warranted, she throws,
which, caught by me in conscience, signify.

Where she most blossoms, stand I in her sight?
Do I deserve her givings, such to share?
How wretched, then, to bait her sanguine air
with teasings unforgivable and trite!

For she, to me both lover and as wife,
compels my soul, more precious than my life.

Tears in Autumn

The dying shades of Autumn richly shown
in beaten copper, burnished gold-leaf bright.
Dried curls of auburn from the branches blown
to drifts of russet-red in fading light.

Remembering her smile then made him groan,
her summer laughter vanished without trace.
With shortening days, the swallows long since flown,
he ached with thoughts of her in warm embrace.

But she had left, that stole his heart, like thief,
her eyes to richer, nobler men now shone.
Cast off, too dull, he shrank in single grief,
earth-bound and lost, his fickle lover gone.

The tears fell silent down his empty face,
forgot by one who ran a faster race.

First Person Singular

She's packed and gone, and I'm left on my own,
she said I'd changed and must reap what I'd sown.
Licking my wounds from her flesh-cutting tongue,
life was once sweet, ah, but then we were young.

'Selfish', she said, 'like a child over-grown.'
'Always', I said, 'you find fault, nag and moan.'
To old excuses I stubbornly clung,
I knew she was right, my nerves over-strung.

'Why can't you come home?' 'I feel so alone!'
'You gnaw my head like a dog with a bone!'
My last dried-up meal in the dustbin flung,
the party over, the song had been sung.

'Come back, my love, cross my heart, I'll atone.'
'For God's sake, I'm trying, pick up the phone!'

Reflection

Yours were the ears when all the world was deaf,
you were the tongue that spoke to me at night.
The arms that caught me when I fell were yours,
and yours the eyes that made the darkness bright.

I was the one that woke in nightmare's grip,
mine were the sad and angry bitter tears.
My wounded heart your understanding healed,
and helped me swim through thoughts of drowning fears.

You were the time that paused whilst I caught up,
yours were the hands that soothed my troubled head.
The pain I felt was recognised by you,
and you the calm when nothing need be said.

I learned again to smile and be at peace,
resolved to start again, a second chance.
Encouraged, strengthened, lifted out of gloom,
reach out to light, the rhythm of the dance.

Supported by our children's knowing looks,
we held each other's hand in joining vows,
We live for both, and all that near us are,
and hope that life a little more allows.

Messages

Rolled up vellum, dried-on ink,
pledging romance, heavens brink.
Scrolling letters, patient hand,
blotting paper, drying sand.
Sharpened goose quill, pewter pot,
candle dripping, wax sealed hot.
Indecision, words unkind,
lies discovered, change of mind.
Broken promise, moment lost,
torn asunder, dog-grate tossed.

Writing paper, Parker blue,
marriage promise, ever true.
Thoughtful sentence, might coerce,
cartridge re-fill, words in verse.
Non-committal, can't decide,
other lover, on the side.
Truth avoiding, with intent,
wasted effort, time ill spent.
Patience ended, wasn't right,
put through shredder, out of sight.

Plastic mobile, options pressed,
found on website, overstressed.
Cyber café, meeting place,
relationship, in your face.
Live together, for a while,
break up with no reconcile.
Declaring war, spitting hate
meet in court, apportionate.
One text message, indiscreet,
"C U L8er?".....press delete.

- Prose and Past -

Bowl

On the news I saw a city, somewhere in the world.
In the middle of the city was a fabulous, modern building.
It was tall and elegant, all glass and stainless steel,
Inside, the floors were clad in vast sheets of polished marble.
There were crystal chandeliers, and doors of precious wood.
Outside, in a circle, round the building were many flags,
Curling proudly from just as many white, exact poles.
The flags were the rainbow colours of many nations.
In front of the bullet-proof doors were many steps
leading down to a large, man-made lake.
In the middle of the lake was a great fountain.
The fountain never stopped, it was full of life.
Then I watched as many shiny limousines arrived.
Out of them emerged important looking people in well-cut, dark clothes.
They shook hands with each other, and smiled with well-fed faces.
Burly security men with lumpy jackets stood in rows.
Hordes of photographers rushed forward with expensive cameras.
Gradually, the building filled up with all these well-paid people,
well-intentioned, but with feeble consciences.
Next day the papers would be full of the news.
Full of empty, bold promises.
Again.

Next week the building will be empty.
But the echoes of many speeches will remain.
The Ministers, Ambassadors, Attachés, interpreters,
secretaries, security-men, caterers, and even the pressmen,
will all have gone home for the weekend.
There will only be a handful of cleaners
to polish the echoes of the meeting.
to dust the wasteful building, full of words,
and empty the full waste-bins of shredded paper.
The flags will still laze crazily from the poles.
Useless emblems, full of pride.
A pointless fountain, used by no-one, '
but landscaped, nevertheless.
One of the cleaners may switch on a radio.
It might play an old song, *"Life is just a bowl of cherries."*

Later, on the same news programme, I saw another place.
A small village, somewhere in the world.
Squalid and pathetic, all neglected and near ruin.
There were many people sitting and lying around.
Their bodies were starved and they stared with haunted faces.
They wore little, or nothing, and were waiting to die.
Some lived in hovels, with bare, earth floors,
living in filth and squalor, infested with insects and vermin.
Their roofs were old, rusty, corrugated iron
hanging sadly on flimsy, rotten timbers.
Others had small, old canvas tents, or bits of plastic sheets,
hurriedly sent from a struggling charitable organisation.
Nearby were a few steps leading down to an old well.
It had dried up weeks ago, the water had stopped.
Some men with shiny rifles stood scowling.
Their jeep was boastfully flying a small, unknown flag.
A camera-man walked nervously around,
filming an earnest reporter speaking animated words.
Nearby was a small child with huge eyes and limbs like twigs,
carrying an empty wooden bowl.
Next day, the papers would be full of this typical, boring news.
Again.

Next week it will still be the same.
Though the graves of many of the people will be new.
The barren ground will be full of their bones,
dark parchment stretching over them,
hastily buried in their rags, barely covered with sand.
There will be no echoes, for there were no words.
The sheets of rusty iron, canvas and plastic will still flap angrily
until the pitiless, dry winds blow them away to the next landscape.

These are the emblems I hate.
Emblems of pride and emblems of poverty.
Rows of crazy, useless flags, hanging beautifully.
Rows of starved, stinking bodies, rotting silently.
A man-made fountain, landscaped and undrinkable.
A hand-dug well, miserable and thirsty.
A concrete palace, full of fine words.
A bowl, full of nothing.

The Four Hills of 'Glutton Grange'

Earl Sterndale

There are four hills at Glutton Grange.
Each one a different size, shape and character.
I have been in their shadow all my life.
They have sheltered my nights and reflected my days,
delighted all my senses, and drained my sweat.
Farming on them, they have fed my stock, and therefore, me.
By them, I've lived and worked, laughed and cried, awake and asleep.
My legs have climbed them, up and down, over many seasons.
My arms have heaved new hay on their fertile slopes,
scythed thistles, dug ditches, and axed logs for Christmas.
My hands have tickled trout in the cool, clear river Dove
that flows through their lush, lower meadows;
I have mended old limestone walls, which were built and rebuilt
by seven generations of my surname in this parish of Earl Sterndale.
I have been privileged to help many a struggling cow and ewe
to give birth in the quiet times of the night,
when the mad, rushing world seemed so far away.
I have witnessed bright, green, fickle Springs, the rich prime of Summers,
glowing, sad Autumn times and bitter Winter blizzards.
The encircling mass of these four hills have been a constant companion to me.
They have made me reflect, both in quiet joy, and in occasional disappointment,
made plans for a future that didn't always happen, but was worthwhile trying for.
Felt safe in troubled times, and appreciated their special hold on me.
They have revealed their myriad forms of life and changing rhythms to me;
furtive wild animals, the hum of insects, and the return of swallows.
The cycle of leaves, rich and ruined harvests, wild winds, magical dawns,
eerie, lonely mists and sunsets to make artists weep, and writers dumb.
I can say I have never looked around these hills with boredom once,
Or ever seen the same sky above them twice,

On two of the four hills are very tangible ancient records of Man
in the form of circular limestone tumuli of the Beaker People.
The sense of belonging and human continuation in this place
could not be more vivid, as my eyes look out over the same hills
that those early men gazed on in their primal wonderings.
The hills' curious form, fossil-rich from pre-historic coral seas,
are no less alive today than they were then, just in a different age.
When I was a young boy, I used to imagine the four hills were people.
Four huge, vital, magical giants of differing ages from long, long ago.
That early image has stayed, and even developed, with me.

160

The smallest hill, right behind the farm, is called 'Sohum' hill.
It is, and I hope always will be, pronounced "Sorms".
This one always seemed like a child in my mind, a Child of the Ancients.
Partly chubby, but old enough to run on sturdy legs and hide.
This little, squat hill stretches and runs up into a quiet, hidden dale.
This spurt of growth, from early childhood to adolescence,
seems to signify the first quarter of life; the adventure begins.

'Parkhouse' hill is the next in the cycle. Tall, proud, fearless,
a warrior, keen to prove himself and make his mark.
Clad in badger-skins, with long, black hair blowing in the wind.
Sharp-eyed, and hungry, like the kestrel hovering over the steep grassy slopes,
hanging menacingly in the lifting breeze drawn up by little cliffs and pinnacles.
'Parkhouse' is a young hunter that struggled and survived.
Conquest, thrill of the chase, pride in being accepted by his woman and fellow men.
Surprised by his new-found tenderness, but not prepared to give up his roar.
He is full of strength and eager, emblem of the second stage of life.

The third hill is called 'Glutton', though it is also known as 'Round' hill.
 Expansive in shape, domed, seeming slightly overweight and smiling.
This hill has a wide circular base and a raised umbrella of spherical mass.
In my imagination this always seemed like a late-middle-aged man;
mature, knowing, encouraging, yet anxious for his children's falterings,
remembering his own mistakes, and showing tolerance because of that.
A defensible place, secure, generous and guarding, like a father-figure.
The third part of the circle. A consolidation of the provider, with experience,
some proud scars of success, lines of worry, toil, and wisdom intermingling.

Lastly comes 'Hitter' hill. The Old One. Wrinkled, waiting, content.
Remembering battles, won and lost, regretting some things, not others.
Preparing for the last long journey of oblivion. The Sage.
Leaving only the ring of stones of the burial place,
and the vibrant blood of the later generations as testament of his being.
His last deed linked inexorably to the strivings of tomorrow's youth.

My father's ashes lie scattered over Parkhouse.
I have instructed my family to do the same for me one day.
My son says he will go there also.
These hills nurture you, and then they let you go on your adventure,
But they call you back.

Be still, and lie with the old ones.
When you are ready.

A new place

I awake, and it is still dark.
They say the darkest hour is just before dawn,
yet I have forgotten what dawn is like.
Here, in my small world of blackness there is no dawn.
I have forgotten what light is like.
So I close my eyes again, and yet it is no darker.
I have almost forgotten who I am,
but never can I forget my darkness,
this blackness is all mine.
Here is my place.
No light.

I try to remember what sound snow makes.
Why do trees move their arms in silence?
What tastes yellow? Does the sun shout?
Can you smell silk? What colour is retribution?
How loud is a moth? Do rocks sing?
My senses blur and my head aches with too much reasoning,
but I have time and blackness on my side.
So I try and unravel this screaming kaleidoscope in my brain;
the half-faces, the quarter places, the eighth voices,
the sixteenth colours and thirty-secondths of time.
I turn the toy – click! – another pattern, another age.
How short is a year?
When shall I see again,
rise up and fly?
Where from?
What to?

My blackness round me is all-pervading,
and drowns my thoughts in comfortable pain.
I crawl into my darkness and spin my cocoon of silence,
suspended here on a thread of life.
My little place, this black space
I know so well.
Still life.

Victim of circumstance, a misfortunate mistake,
an experiment of men's ways, some justifiable reason.
Their calculated scapegoat is my chronicle of wasted time.
A speck in eons.
No matter.

I shall give them silence and let them have their say.
My darkness is deaf, blind, tasteless and dumb,
my silence has no odour.
I lie still in a senseless animation.

One more time I turn the kaleidoscope – click!
Another pattern, another age.
What now?

Suddenly, I sense my friends coming!
I hear their voices, I feel their hands
Coaxing my body to rise up, and taste the air!
To break out and shed my outer casing,
to cut the hanging thread of my cocoon!
My friends are rescuing me out of my blackness,
I am coming to a new place!
I finally decide to open my eyes and see.
They are bringing me to a new place.
I want to sing and fly.

But…I cannot see it,
The blackness seems even darker now,
closer, crushing round my head.
Have I been deceived?
I hear my friends nod.
I smell the quietness tight around my throat.

Turn the toy – click.
I taste the sweet trapdoor,
instantly I sing and fly,
and know the light!

Christchurch to Kaikoura

The red light was flashing on the telephone cradle. A message received.

Not bothering to listen, he threw down his briefcase and rang the 'Mackenzie', giving his name in a voice that suddenly didn't sound like his.

"Its Mr. Curtis, I'm ringing about my wife, Jean Curtis. She's in the Intensive Care Unit, well, ..she was on Ward Seven...but...."

His mouth dried.

"Of course, Mr. Curtis," answered the calm, well-trained receptionist, "I'll put you through to Ward Seven, its Nurse Sharon you need to speak to, please hold."

He said to himself, she'll answer with that "Hi, Intensive Care Unit, Nurse Sharon speaking. Can I help you?" using that cheerful, bright, West-Coaster twang of hers that grated, and yet was so comforting in its normality.

"Hi, Nurse Sharon spea..."

"Sharon, it's John Curtis," he interrupted, "how is she?"

"Mr. Curtis, Jean has been moved into a side ward and she is asking for you. I think it best to tell you that you really do need to be here, things are not too good right now. Can you get someone to drive you over..."

"On my way," he said hoarsely, and dropped the receiver down as if it were burning. He grabbed his overnight bag, already packed, slammed the door shut and ran down the path to the shabby, old Austin.

"Come on, one more time. Don't let me down. This is the last.... *please*...."

He prayed to some unknown deity as he pulled the choke and turned the ignition. His eyes narrowed and looked past the bonnet with the flying 'A' mascot, focusing on something in the distance that wasn't there.

The Port hills rose up behind the broad sprawl of Christchurch city, their slopes purpling and vermilion in the hot late-afternoon.

Whoever is was up there took pity on him as the temperamental Austin sputtered into life. Soon he was heading north up the coast road beside the oblivious, rolling Southern Pacific.

He thought of her and though he tried he couldn't blot out the ashen colour she had become. Underneath the horrible, light-green hospital sheet, her emaciated body, the swollen stomach, her skin like ecru.

Alongside the narrow gravel road Rata bushes grew, their silky, luxurious blossoms hanging down in great swags.

They made him think of her and of another time. How could he have forgotten her birthday that time? He never did again.

For most people it was a long drive from Christ Church to Kaikoura. For him, it was becoming the shortest journey; an automatic action, with time seeming to stand still in between each place. He gripped the steering wheel and cried out aloud in an

164

animal howl at the futility and absolute vitalness of his pilgrimage. How often had he made this nightmare ride? It didn't matter anyhow, it never mattered.

The car rattled over long, wooden, trestle bridges that spanned North Canterbury's wide rivers, their waters clear and still cold from the glaciers they had started from only days ago.

It was our wedding night; we were going to live forever!

The road threaded the rocky shore, leaving sight of the ocean occasionally where the grey granite became too towering and precipitous. Ancient Pohutakawa trees clung impossibly to the steep slopes, their fiery, scarlet flowers carpeting whole sections of the road like Turkish rugs. The same red as her wedding dress had been.

We were dancing! Dancing in a sea of smiles!

The perfume filled the dry summer air as he pushed the accelerator to its complaining maximum. In front of him a couple of Kea parrots flew across the valley; their drab olive-green plumage lit up by the vibrant orange of the under-feathers beneath their wings. Why was there always two of everything? That was just natural. Ironically, he felt so desperately caged and they were so free. He felt an ugly jealousy and hated himself for it. He liked keas really

He imagined her waiting for him. All his senses were tense and jarring. He almost wanted this journey to be a never-ending pact, a promise to fulfil. A promise since…how long ago? He had made this drive for the last four months. A diligent pilgrimage focused to one purpose - that she would live. She had to live.

The automatic change-over between the two places of home and hospice was transitory, arbitrary. He'd sometimes stayed in a motel nearby the 'Mackenzie', but then his work and responsibilities were impossible to leave for more than a couple of days.

Now the countryside became gentler, the road straighter and faster.

Coming through the clumps of cabbage trees that flanked the far end of the rolling plain the land began to rise up.

There she was, taking photographs! The children were laughing!

At the top of the hill he stopped for a moment to let the car cool down. Steam had been wisping from the bonnet for a good few miles now. He lit a cigarette and waited till he dare try the rusty radiator cap.

To the left, the coastal range spread far to the north, their snow-capped peaks burning pink in the last half-hour of sunset. On his right the sparkling surfs of the gleaming ocean. Where the calm land met the boiling sea seemed to personify their two lives. He threw the empty water canister into the boot and bludgeoned on over the dusty escarpment. He felt cruelly cheated. They had only had half their lives. She had to live.

Suddenly, below, the little town of Kaikuora lay waiting. He was near the end of the journey. Had he really been driving for almost.... how many hours? It didn't matter, it never mattered.

She was waiting for him, dying to tell him the conveyance had come through!

She was waiting. The urgent, agonizing meeting-place was waiting. A side ward of a hospice. The last place he ever thought she would be waiting for him.

Where would you choose for a last meeting?

With nerves screeching he drove down to the hospital entrance and was appalled to hear himself cry out "I'm here! I'm here! Wait for me!"

Wait! Don't run so fast! You've longer legs than me!

'McKenzie Hospice' said the bland, impersonal sign. It was the final, impossible rendezvous, the most vicious and kindest place to say good-bye.

Hello, I'm back!

Although he ached desperately to go quickly into the building, he steeled himself to dry his eyes, breathe deep, become calm, try an encouraging smile, and be stupidly brave. He paused to look at his watch to get a sense of something, anything...time, place, distance, hope, and ordinariness. It was five minutes to eight.

It's nearly eight o'clock, you're going to be late!

He knew this time would be earth-shattering, untouchable....like they always had been. He felt gripped, crushed in the pain and finality of it all.

Pushing open the light-coloured doors, He crossed over to the reception area in a daze, and then on down to the Intensive Care section.

Nurse Sharon smiled compassionately at him as he entered. Without speaking she took his arm, lead him to the side-room door, eased him so very gently inside, silently checked the morphine drip, and left.

How do you think I feel? It's alright for you, you're not always here!

Jean lay with her eyes open. She was staring through the window. The panorama was superb. On one side was the old harbour, and beyond the break-water, the waves rolling relentlessly in. Further round was the volcanic mass of the jagged Kaikoura range, on fire with the setting sun. It was beautiful.

Let's go to Kaikoura, I love the crayfish there!

166

He felt his head sing with recollections and dreaded anticipation. He sat down quietly on the chair beside her and took her cool, dry, thin hand.

"Hello you," he said simply.

"Hello, you! Had a good day?"

"How are you feeli...."
"Did you enjoy the drive?" she whispered, interrupting and ignoring his question, changing the subject for his sake.
Memories whirled across his brain. Not of the drive.
"The drive was truly magnificent, but not as lovely as you are. I love you," he said, "but you know that, don't you?"
She drifted away for some moments, and then came back. The peace was serene, yet hideous. There, before him, was the dearest person in his life. Dying.
"Yes,... thank you." she said gently, hardly audible, slowly blinking her eyes.

I'm dying to tell you! Guess what!

In a glass vase on the bedside cabinet the Rata blooms he had brought for her yesterday glowed a deep red.
The second finger of the wall clock moved round silently, unremittingly.
The morphine drip let fall its tiny globule of compassion.

Don't you remember that time? When we waited ages in Kaikoura!

She moved her head very slightly, closed her eyes, and whispered,

"I... love... y...."

Her breathing became shallower, and slower, paused ...and stopped.

His heart pounded in utter grief,
and was then the only sound in the room.

Morning Rain

A conscious faint drumming of finest rain,
the hissing sound of weather's tinnitus.
White opals drip, drip, drip, along the plain
iron railings of a varnished fire escape.
As drop, drop, drop the soaking pearls' strung drape,
to shock the waiting puddle's glassy plane
in regular minute tsunami,
and, oh, the peace of it, this morning rain!

A limpid, sad sheen glosses, bends the trees,
cascades a canopy irregular,
to add more drenching to the drowning earth.
Some blackbird's clear, full-hearted coda weaves
a threnody between the boughs, and leaves
its spirit to this distillation's dearth.
On emerald grass, rich gems spun globular,
green facets in a shining swell of seas.

Translucent mass of cloudy hanging grey,
impenetrable to the higher blue,
a stranglehold on urging push of dawn.
Ritual of morning pride's delusion
liquefies and takes in smooth transfusion
the clearing air, silk-soothed and cleansed. Re-born
in pausing moment of my life's review.
Relieves the sorrows from a distant day.

Even though the saturation over,
still comes the sound, re-echoed on again,
memory reminds my ear's affliction
ringing, ringing in a sour annoyance.
When, in future time, this loathsome noise grants
peace, then I'll remember with affection
the calm of that still singing, singing rain.
Oh, that morning, and it's blackbird lover!

On hearing The Aquarelle Guitar Quartet play their arrangement of 'Palhaço',
by Egberto Gismonti, at The Palace Hotel, Buxton. - The Buxton Festival, 2009.

Palhaço

Lugubriously,
a sickly grin spreads wide across his face.
The mirror tells him what he lacks and must re-paint;
his single teardrop.

Palette of make-up,
the careful outline penciled on his cheek.
A black-rimmed pool, and yet his doleful eyes are dry,
tragi-comedy.

His doubled image,
veneer of surface-sorrow, hides the depth.
The grease-paint-grief complete, his art suspends belief,
defies gravity.

Alone in his room,
he thinks of the crowd gathering to pay.
Brief humour of his misfortune helps to mask their own,
their hearts on his sleeve.

His show must go on,
each night a new teardrop, which never falls,
sorrow trapped behind the mirror he cannot break.
"Vesti la giubba!"

Palhaço – clown

"On with the motley!"

Bluetit

In you sweep, yellow-blue gnat,
live pendant of enamel,
hanging, busily flitching
this way and that way………Your blue and lemon twitch,
                small droplet of busy-ness,
                clutching up-side-down
                from clasp of wired feet……Snow is your perfect foil,
                                dull velvet to your show,
                                your blur of busy colour
                                well set to advantage........

Eye, bead, a tiny jet,
the small closed fan
of your tail goes
that way, this way………….A busy blueness
                and lemon flittering,
                stab of beaked purpose.
                Suddenly, you're gone……...The trees are stilled,
                                black, snow-spun,
                                frost anaesthetized,
                                winter suspended………

Busily back you come,
bullying the feeder
to swing and yield,
sway-this-way-that……….. Atom acrobat
                of bird-business,
                lemon-flicked,
                blue-blurred…………………..And away.
                                I didn't
                                even see
                                you go…………………..

        t
        w
        i   f
        t   l   t
        c   i   i
        h   t   t

170

Old Dogs

She's tired, and kind,
with drooping ears which hang uneven,
spattered coat of colour, white and nearly red,
the troublesome foreleg never properly set,
the one she puts out to the left.

Reliant on each other,
how often she spends her day,
never far from my hand,
whistled away, come by, walk on.

Running through my memories,
soft buried in my heart

He's wired and blind,
the realism whose beads are lost,
indeterminate colour, pale brown if anything,
sawdust creeps from front and back,
worn sacking, warp and weft.

Close to my smiles and tears,
the stitched nose overlay,
never far from my hand,
mainly off the bed, and sometimes on.

Comfort of childhood,
never really growing old.

Two old dogs,

such parts of my life.

- *Publications & Data* -

"*Selected Poems*" 2004

"*More Poems*" 2005

"*Poetry Times Three*" 2006

"*Fourth in Line*" 2007

"*Words of the White Peak*" The Disappearing Dialect of a Derbyshire Village, 2008
ISBN 9781898670155
Foreword by Her Grace, The Dowager Duchess of Devonshire.

"*Words of a Derbyshire Poet*" A Collection, 2009
ISBN 9781898670155
Foreword by Sir Christopher Ball.

All the books are available from either:
'Mayfield Books and Gifts', 9. Orgreave Close, Handsworth, Sheffield, S13 9NP
Tel: 01142 889 522 , Fax: 01142 691 499
Or directly from the Author : philipholland@uwclub.net

"*The Girl with Auburn Hair*" Op.14, and "*Once*" Op.42, in "*Selected Poems*" 2004,
were both chosen and exhibited for three weeks in 'The Oxo Tower' and 'The
Bargehouse', on the South Bank, London, in the London Art Co.'s '*Art of Love*'
Competition in 2004.

"*The Coot*" Op.48, in "*More Poems*" 2005, was also published in The Derbyshire
County Community Anthology – "*Arnemetiae*", 2005.

"*Four*" Op.107, in "*Fourth in Line*" 2007, was also published in the Norwich Writers'
Circle Open Poetry Competition's Anthology, 2007.

"*The Gather*" Op.76, in "*Poetry Times Three*" 2007, won Joint First Prize in The
Huddersfield Literary Festival's Open Poetry Competition in March, 2007.

"*The Gather*" was also published in "*The North*" Poetry Magazine, June Ed., 2007.

"*Words of the White Peak*" The Disappearing Dialect of a Derbyshire Village, 2008
was featured on B.B.C. Radio 4 in the '*Today*' programme with John Humphrys,
B.B.C. Radio 5, B.B.C. East Midlands T.V., B.B.C. North West T.V., Manchester
Evening News Channel 'M' T.V., Radio Derby and High Peak Radio.

- *Reviews & Information* -

"Now we can begin to see the development of his own authentic voice speaking about the things which interest him; the countryside, as expected from someone who has spent the greater part of his life farming; music, as also expected from a fine musician, but other sources as well, ranging from a pair of curtains to a pair of rhinos in South Africa. Philip reads his poetry with a quiet confidence which is most attractive. The addition of musical excerpts introducing and closing the poems, and sometimes between the verses, serves to point up the particular quality of each poem and heightens our enjoyment."

Peter Low, 2005

"Philip's poetry is quarried from his Derbyshire and flows with the unconscious, natural speech rhythms and dialect of this locality. The theme of natural change is celebrated with a sense of security about our place in time, using contemplative, perceptive poems that make you respond with a wry smile of recognition, or laugh out loud with shared appreciation and understanding. The diversity of the poetry is entertaining: an amusing allegorical free verse about the life of a pair of shoes; a parody of a rhyming poem John Betjeman might have penned on a wet High Street; to my personal favourite, "The Gather", a poem that works like a riddle and is full of the fresh voice of a new poet sharing a moment of heightened emotion."

Alyson Phillips, 2007

"Philip Holland delivers, with feeling and gusto, a rich variety of poetry in differing styles, structure and content, from the serious to the silly. There was something to please everyone whether it be to provoke a smile or make you ponder, interspersed with appropriate snippets of well played piano pieces. There was love, tragedy, dialect, animals, and the weather drawn from life's experiences, which I was able to relate to immediately. Simple titles belied the depth of observation of their author. Recommended whether you know Philip's poetry or not, you simply must hear a 'disappearing poem' of what happened on the wedding night of two three-toed sloths!"

Nicola Stacey, 2009

Please feel free to visit the website: www.fphiliphollandpoetry.co.uk
The author is available to give Poetry Readings and Recitals, punctuated with live piano music, for all kinds of Societies, Clubs, Organisations and private functions. Please email to request details: philipholland@uwclub.net

- *References and Bibliography* -

p.118 **Arbor Low**. Constructed circa 2,500 B.C., this Neolithic Stone Age site is regarded as the third most important in England after Stonehenge and Avebury. Together with its 'sister henge', 'The Bull Ring', a few miles away at Dove Holes, Arbor Low is a fascinating enigma. At 1,200 feet above sea level, it consists of a high, circular earth mound around a wide inner ditch, which in turn encloses a round, level 'sanctuary' area. There are also 46 huge and 13 lesser stones circularly arranged flat, as opposed to the more typical upright position, in this inner area. Two later-constructed barrows lie outside the main circles.

p.91 **Auschwitz**. Refers to Auschwitz III, (Monowitz). Named after the polish village of Monowice, this Nazi slave-labour camp was where Mr. Denis Avey was held prisoner. The factories here were associated with munitions, foundries and mining. Also in the production of synthetic rubber and liquid fuel by the '*Buna-Werke*', which was owned by the Nazi-sympathetic I. G. Farben. The inmates were subjected to extreme hard labour, very meagre rations and terrible punishments. Although the exact figures murdered in the Holocaust as a whole may never be known, conservative estimates put the total number of genocidal and other killings in all the Nazi-run extermination centres as between 7,000,000 to 8,000,000. Although predominantly Jews, those also annihilated included Romas, political dissidents, intelligentsia, artists, religious variants, homosexuals, and the physically and mentally ill.

p.68 **Bach,** Johann Sebastian, 1685 – 1750. Acknowledged as the greatest Baroque era composer. He was highly prolific in all the musical forms and genres of his age and was also a brilliant organist. There are well over 1,000 known compositions by him; orchestral, choral, organ, harpsichord, string ensembles, single voice and most solo instruments. The Bach family is one which boasts a number of fine composers and musicians, but J. S. Bach is usually regarded as 'The Father of Music'. He wrote six "*English Suites*" in total.

p.113 **Beckett**, Samuel, 1906 – 1989. Irish poet, playwright and critic. His most famous absurdist play, *"Waiting for Godot",* was premiered at the 'Théâtre de Babylone', Paris, in 1953. Once described as "…*a play in which nothing happens, twice*" this tragi-comedy was also once voted as "…*the most significant play of the 20 th century.*" On a stark stage set, two men, Vladimir and Estragon, wait for Godot, who never appears. Inertia, boots, religion, hats, psychology, carrots, suicide threats, loneliness, and several more odd characters, one being the hapless 'Lucky', occur in a strange mix of whimsical paralysis, qua paranoia. The play could be described as both inanimation in vacuum and ennui in perpetuum.

p.40 **Bernini**, Giovanni Lorenzo, 1598 - 1680. Born in Naples, his prodigious works dominated 17th Century sculpture and architecture in Rome and beyond. His famous double statue, "*The Rape of Proserpina*", depicting Pluto forcibly carrying off Proserpina into the Underworld, was sculpted between 1621-1622. The dramatic composition is made even more malevolent with Cerberus, the three-headed dog, guarding the struggling protagonists.

p.43 **Boccaccio**, Giovanni, 1313 – 1375. Italian Renaissance author and poet. He lived most of his life, intermittently, in Certaldo in Tuscany. Some sources claim he was born there. "*The Decameron*", arguably the most famous book written by him, tells of three

174

young men and seven young women who flee to Certaldo to escape the plague in Florence. They while away the time by each one telling a story every day for ten days.

p.68 **Chopin**, Fryderyk, Franciszek, 1810 – 1849. Polish composer and virtuoso pianist. This brilliant musician is well-known for his challenging compositions. He is particularly famous for his nocturnes, ballades, scherzos, études, mazurkas, impromptus, preludes and waltzes. He was once romantically linked with the bohemian French authoress, Baroness Dudevant, better known as George Sand. He died in Paris from tuberculosis, and, though buried in the Père Lachaise Cemetery, his heart was returned to his beloved native Poland.

p.164 **Christchurch**. Locally known as '*The Garden City*', this second-largest urban area of New Zealand is situated north of the Banks Peninsula on the East coast of the South Island. Its main river is the Avon and the city is served by the port of Lyttleton. The first Europeans landed in Canterbury in 1815, some 45 years after Captain James Cook first sighted 'Banks Island', which later turned out to be a peninsula. In 1893, New Zealand 'suffragettes', led by Kate Sheppard, secured the right to vote, a World first for women.

p.138 **Coleridge**, Samuel Taylor, 1772 - 1834. English '*Romantic*' poet, literary critic and philosopher. With Robert Southey, he tried to found, unsuccessfully, a utopian commune known as '*Pantisocracy*' in Pennsylvania. With Wordsworth, he published '*Lyrical Ballads*' in 1798. One of Coleridge's best-known poems, "*The Rime of the Ancient Mariner*" occurs in this joint collection. His narrative poem, "*Kubla Khan*", written in 1798, is said to have been composed during and after an opium-induced dream.

p.68 **Congreve**, William, 1670 - 1729. Acknowledged as the greatest English Restoration dramatist. His comedies comment brilliantly on the social and moral modes of his time, culminating in his acknowledged masterpiece, "*The Way of the World*", written in 1700. The quote on p.68 comes from his only tragedy "*The Mourning Bride*", written in 1697.

p.17 **Culloden**. This last major battle on British soil was fought on April 16th, 1746. The French-supported Jacobite Rebellion, led by '*Bonnie Prince Charlie*', (Prince Charles Edward Stuart, also known as *The Young Pretender*), tried to re-establish the Stuart Dynasty but was defeated by the Royal Army of the reigning British Hanoverian monarch, George II.

p.17 **Cumberland**. Refers to The Duke of Cumberland, younger son of George II. He commanded his father's Army at the above battle. Though victorious against the Catholic Jacobite Rebellion, he was certainly guilty of ordering vicious atrocities to both wounded and captured Highlanders, earning him the ignominious title of '*Butcher Cumberland*'.

p.28 **Cyclops**. One of a race of numerous mythical one-eyed giants. Many ancient writers and poets, including Hesiod, Euripides Theocritus and Virgil tell of these monsters. Probably the most well-known of these Cyclopes is Polyphemus, son of Poseidon and Thoosa, as recounted by Homer in his immortal "*Odyssey*".

p.83 **Daemon**. The name of the Monster created by Doctor Victor Frankenstein in Mary Shelley's gothic masterpiece, "*Frankenstein*". Subtitled "*The Modern Prometheus*", it was written when she was only 18 years old, and published anonymously in 1818. Born Mary Wollstonecraft, (she later became the wife of Percy Bysshe Shelley), her book explores the making of a hideous monster by a scientist playing the role of God. It juxtaposes the ancient story of Prometheus, who steals fire from the Gods and gives it to Mankind. Prometheus is punished by the Gods by being chained to a rock and eternally tortured by birds devouring his liver, which constantly regenerates.

p.49 **Darwin,** Charles Robert, 1809 - 1882. English anthropologist, scientist and free thinker. On a five year world-wide voyage in *H.M.S. Beagle*, Darwin finally crystallized his research and ideas during a stay on The Galapagos Islands. He then published his radical "*On the Origin of Species by Means of Natural Selection*", in 1859. Though a shocked public, and an even more antagonistic Church, reviled his theories, the term '*Darwinism*' is still universally recognised as one of the most important studies of evolution.

p.114 **Eunoia**. Greek etymological word meaning "*beautiful thinking*". Also the title of a uni-vowel prose book in this genre by the Canadian poet, Christian Bök, published in 2001.

p.35 **Fitzgerald**, Edward, 1809 - 1883. English poet and first translator of "*The Rubáiyát of Omar Khayyám*" The Persian poet known as Omar Khayyám, 1048 - 1123, who was also a mathematician and astronomer, reputedly wrote over 1,000 *rubais*, (four line verses). These were popularised in Victorian times after several people had made translations of them, with varying success. Not all literary critics agree to the merit or validity of them, but Edward Fitzgerald's were, arguably, the best. A '*rubai*' poem has a rhyming scheme *a, a, b, a.*

p.169 **Gismonti**, Egberto Amin, b.1947. Born in Rio de Janeiro. This virtuoso Brazilian composer, guitarist and pianist studied for some time in Paris with Nadia Boulanger. His popular '*choro*' style can feature both 6 and 10 string guitars. "*Palhaço*" (Clown) is a piece composed by him which has been arranged by many musicians.

p.160 **Glutton Grange,** Derbyshire. Although its painted date-stone declares 1675, the present frontage of this sturdy farmhouse was built nearer a hundred years later, though there are many traces of a much earlier house on the north elevation. At one time a monastic grange, the place is mentioned as '*Glotonhous*' in 1415, and as '*Glatton*' in 1617. The River Dove flows through the lower meadows and on its surrounding hilltops are two good examples of early Beaker People tumuli. The coral reef limestone hills make a very scenic aspect, and a well-known 'double sunset' occurs on Parkhouse Hill at the Summer solstice. F. Philip Holland farmed here for forty years. There have been seven continuous generations of his family to farm in the parish of Earl Sterndale.

p.92 **Hannibal**, 247 - 182 B.C. Renowned as one of the most brilliant military Generals, he was born in Carthage, a son of Hamilcar Barca. During the Second Punic War, Hannibal crossed from Iberia with 38,000 infantry, 8,000 cavalry and 37 war elephants over both The Pyrenees and The Alps to invade the Roman heartland. He rampaged around the country for 15 years. One of his main victories was at The Battle of Trasimene, where he cleverly out-manoeuvred and defeated the Roman legions under Flaminius, inflicting terrible losses.

176

p.72 **Hannibal** Lecter. Psychotic serial killer and cannibal. The character portrayed by Anthony Hopkins in the 1991 film *"The Silence of the Lambs"*, based on the novel by Thomas Harris. A famous quote; "I ate his liver with some fava beans and a nice Chianti."

.123 **Hardy**, Thomas, 1840 - 1928. English novelist and poet. Hardy published over 1,000 poems and 14 novels. His main themes were set in his beloved Wessex, an area from earlier times, in the South and West of England. His novels, *"Tess of the d'Urbervilles"* 1891, and *"Jude the Obscure"*, 1895, examined marriage, morals and the 'fallen woman' themes, which shocked prim Victorian sensibilities. His short poem, *"The Breaking of Nations"*, written in 1915, succinctly demonstrates his typically sorrowful and bucolic musings.

p.36 **Herewini**. One of the last 19th Century ethnic *'Tohungas'* (chisel tattooists), who lived on the East Coast, New Zealand. The *'moko'*, (chin tattoo), was outlawed by the *'Pakeha'*, (white man), in the late 1800s. In the early days during inter-tribal Maori wars, forcible tattooing of enslaved enemies was carried out. Sometimes these be-headed trophies were sold to European traders. Maoris are famed for their intimidating *'Hakas'* (war challenges).

p.84 **Holbein**, Hans, The Younger, 1497 - 1543. Born in Augsburg, this German painter and print-maker achieved probably the supreme 'portrait of propaganda' ever, in his portrayal of Henry VIII in 1537. The dissipated Tudor monarch was only ten years from his death, and yet was shown as his former majestic, virile self, a symbol of power and wealth. The term, 'artistic licence' was paid for to be suitably impressive. Another well-known picture by Holbein is *"The Ambassadors"*, painted in 1533.

p.164 **Kaikoura**. Situated on the East coast of the South Island of New Zealand, this place was originally a whaling station. Ironically, nowadays the place is a tourist centre for whale-watching. The Maori words 'kai koura' mean 'meal of crayfish'. This fishing port still supports a renowned crayfish-producing industry. The coastal mountain range is impressive.

p.74 **King Louis**. King Louis XVI of France, 1754 - 1793. Frivolous behaviour by the aristocracy, bad counsel by nobles, radical political factions and a deepening national decline all brought about The French Revolution which sealed the fate of the glittering court of the Bourbon dynasty. After 'The Storming of The Bastille' on the 14th of July, 1789, the newly-formed National Convention abolished the absolutist Monarchy in September 1792. Louis XVI was executed by guillotine in January the next year.

p.26 & p.54 **Lawrence**, David Herbert, 1885 - 1930. Nottinghamshire-born son of a coal-miner. A controversial writer, Lawrence has come to be regarded as a major influence in English Literature. The famous 'obscene publication' trial concerning his sexually explicit book, *"Lady Chatterley's Lover"*, was a milestone in liberalising literary works. Lawrence was a very widely-travelled man, his book, *"The Plumed Serpent"*, was written in 1926. Although probably better known for his novels and novellas, he was also a fine poet and a talented painter. He also wrote important non-fiction; studies, essays and literary criticism. His poem, *"Mountain Lion"*, was composed in 1923, whilst he was visiting New Mexico. Regarded by some as being misogynistic, Lawrence was deeply attached to his mother. Her influence in his education set him firmly on the road to develop his extraordinary talent.

p.145 **Leda and the Swan**. In Greek mythology the all-powerful god Zeus transforms himself into a swan and seduces Leda. From this union, and also sleeping with her husband, Tyndareus, on the same night, Leda lays two eggs. From these hatch two sets of twins, Helen, Clytemnestra, Castor and Pollux. William Butler Yeats's famous sonnet, *"Leda and the Swan"*, collected in 1928, graphically recounts the erotic story in psychological realism.

p.41 **Loreta.** This Church of Pilgrimage in the Hradcany district of Prague was built by Baroness Beligna Katherina von Lobkowicz in 1626. It has a cloister, a 'holy hut' and the treasury houses many priceless jewelled monstrances. There is also a famous chiming clock with a carillon of 27 bells, constructed in 1695, still functional today. The care of any visiting pilgrims has long been vested with the Capuchin monks.

p.120 **Magpie Mine**. A Derbyshire lead mine situated between the villages of Sheldon and Monyash. Workings there are recorded from 1739 up until its closure in 1958. Its *'Cornish'* engine house and other attendant ruins are vividly prominent at 1,050 feet above sea level on a vast limestone plateau. Underground conflict between rival miners at the nearby Red Soil Mine resulted in the deaths, allegedly murder, of 3 miners in 1833, suffocated by suspect fires lit below the surface. All the shafts have now been 'capped', the deepest one being 222 metres. The local dialect word for a lead-miner was a *'groover'*, the mines being *'grooves'*. Pasture poisoned by lead-working spoils is known as *'belland'* or *'bellanded'* ground.

p.41 **Masada**. An inaccessible mountaintop fortress in Israel developed by King Herod the Great between 37 - 31 B.C. According to the chronicler, Josephus Flavius, besieged Zealots held out here for over two years against the Roman general, Flavius Silva in 72 - 74 A.D. On the eventual capture of the stronghold, it was discovered all the 1,000 or so defenders had committed a systematic suicide pact rather than be enslaved. The heroic event is revered by the Jewish people as the ultimate acts of bravery, independence and commitment.

p.112 **'Mene, mene, tekel, upharsin'**. Known as *'The writing on the wall'*, these words occur in the book of Daniel in the Bible. The Aramaic etymology of these four words translates as *'numbered, numbered, weighed, divided.'* One evening, during a feast at his court, Belshazzar, King of Babylon, watched and read these words prophesying doom mysteriously appear on a wall, written by a disconnected hand. The corrupt Belshazzar was slain the same night and his kingdom was then divided and given to the Medes and Persians.

p.32 **Michelangelo,** di Lodovico Buonarroti Simoni, 1475 - 1564. Supreme painter, sculptor, architect, poet and engineer. He is always synonymous as the other contender for the archetypal 'Renaissance Man' alongside his rival and fellow- Italian, Leonardo da Vinci. Michelangelo's *"Pietà", of 1499,* sculpted in white marble, is in St. Peter's, Rome.

p.112 **Nebuchadnezzar II**, 630 – 562 B.C. An early Babylonian king and also father of the above King Belshazzar. The *"Hanging Gardens of Babylon"*, one of the Seven Wonders of the Ancient World, were reputedly built by Nebuchadnezzar around 600 B.C. as a present for his homesick wife. There are various claims as to the actual site, even the very existence, of the place. However, Nebuchadnezzar II of the Chaldean dynasty certainly existed.

p.35 **Ozymandias**. Another name for Pharoah Rameses II of Egypt. *"Ozymandias"* is also the title of the famous sonnet by Percy Bysshe Shelley, published in 1818. This unusually-formed poem explores the transience of man and the eventual decay of all Empires.

p.43 **Palio di Siena.** This thrilling horse race, which has its roots in medieval times, happens twice a year in Siena on July 2nd and August 16th. Dare-devil jockeys, riding bare-back, try to win and bring honour for one of the seventeen *contrade,* or city wards. Although only ten horses are allowed to run, there is much fierce competition between all the highly partisan supporters in each area. The horses are even taken into the various churches to be blest, and sometimes winning riding helmets may permanently hang in votive thanks.

p.60 **Pavarotti,** Luciano, 1935 - 2007. Undoubtedly the finest tenor of the 20th Century, Pavarotti made his operatic debut as *'Rudolfo'* in Puccini's opera *"La Bohème"* in 1961. Along with José Carreras and Plácido Domingo he will forever be remembered as one of *"The Three Tenors"*. Pavarotti's singing of the aria, *'Nessun Dorma'*, from *'Turandot'*, was made universally popular as the anthem for International Football's 'World Cup' in 1990.

p.47 **Pegasus** - *'The Winged Horse'*. Supposedly born of a union between Poseidon and Medusa, there are various stories about this fantastical beast in Greek mythology. In one, Pegasus was ridden by Bellerophon when he slew the Chimera and also the Amazons.

p.144 **Swainsley Hall**. Built in 1867 by R. Roscoe. Later, home to Sir Thomas Wardle, the silk industry entrepreneur, who also installed an ingenious water-powered organ driven by the River Manifold. Wardle was friendly with William Morris and also had links to The Pre-Raphaelites. Mark Twain, a keen fisherman, was a house-guest during his European tour. Swainsley was enlarged by Admiral Sir Guy Gaunt K.C.M.G. in 1909. Sadly, Lady Gaunt was tragically burnt to death there in 1948. It was later owned by Lt. Col. L. J. Worthington, of Leek, Staffordshire, the third textile mill-owning family to be associated with Swainsley. F. Philip Holland and his family lived there from 1982 – 1994, running it as their home and also as a country house hotel and restaurant.

p.22 **Tennyson,** Alfred Lord, 1809 - 1892. Poet Laureate from 1850 until his death. Probably his best known patriotic poem, *"The Charge of the Light Brigade"*, was published in 1855. There is an early sound recording of Tennyson actually reading it. He was created a Baron in 1884, and is buried in *'Poet's Corner'* in Westminster Abbey. The poem *"Crossing The Bar"* was composed in 1889.

p.36 **Treaty of Waitangi,** signed 1840, between The British Crown and the Maori Chiefs of the North Island, New Zealand. The date of the Treaty is regarded as the 'birth certificate' of New Zealand as a country, though the document is still in dispute by some Maoris. The word, *Waitangi*, means *'sorrowing waters'* in the Maori language.

p.88 **Untermeyer**, Louis, 1885 - 1977. American author, poet, anthologist, and editor. He was co-founder of *"The Seven Arts"* magazine, dedicated to encouraging new poets - one of which was Robert Frost. Untermeyer was awarded a Gold medal by The Poetry Society of America in 1956. His sonnet, *"Portrait of a Machine"*, is a fine example of his talent.